Dan Rice, DVM

Bullmastiffs

Everything About Their Ancestry, Behavior, Care, Nutrition, and Training

Filled with Full-color Photographs
Illustrations by Michele Earle-Bridges

BARRON'S

CONTENTS

ORIGINS OF THE BULLMASTIFF

The Bullmastiff's progenitors (ancestors) and the place and time of its origin are well documented, as is the breed's primary function. The Bullmastiff originated in the middle of the nineteenth century in Great Britain to reduce the poaching problem on private estates' wild game populations.

Canine Contributors

Canines descended from wolves. Some traits of those ferocious and formidable ancestors are genetically wired into the makeup of all domestic dogs. However, to a great degree, genetic behavior is gradually modified through careful breeding and training of dogs that are exposed to certain experiences. All of these factors— genetic background, training, and handling— play a part in forming each Bullmastiff's personality.

Today's Mastiff looks nothing like a contemporary Bulldog. Believe it or not, the Bulldog and Mastiff breeds have each claimed to be the ancestor of the other, but you need a good imagination to adopt that theory. Bulldogs and Mastiffs probably have a common progenitor in the ancient Alaunt, a Great Dane-type giant

A Bullmastiff's gentle expression belies its strength and determination.

that was much taller than today's Bulldog. No matter how they look today, the Bulldog and the Mastiff were definitely the progenitors of the Bullmastiff.

Mastiff

The word *mastiff* is derived from the French word *mastin,* which means "accustomed to the hand." Giant working breeds once were collectively known as Molossian dogs, a term derived from a statue of Molossus, a huge personal bodyguard dog that belonged to Olympias, daughter of Pyrrus, King of Greece, in 400 B.C. Many varieties of giant helper-dogs have been recognized all over the world, many having origin in Asia. Those big guys were often lumped together and called *Mastiffs* regardless of their dissimilar appearances and uses. Some were longhaired herding dogs, others were shorthaired security dogs, but all were huge canines.

At 100 pounds (45 kg) or more, the Bullmastiff is an instinctive watchdog as well as an excellent companion.

Wolves and other dangerous predators were discouraged from harassing Mastiffs' families. That protection extended to human marauders who preyed on the sanctity of English homes. Mastiffs were the most formidable security force in existence among the early English populace. Some English Mastiffs were captured by Roman invaders in about 50 B.C. and taken to Rome where they were pitted against armed men, bulls, bears, lions, and tigers.

Bulldog

The Bulldog originally was bred as a war dog by ancient Britons. In 1500, a writer called it "Bondogge." Later British writers referred to it as "Mastine" or "Bandogge," and sometimes "Butchers Dogge." By about 1630 that purely English breed was commonly referred to as a Bulldog. Early Bulldogs were quite different from those of modern times. They were longer of leg, with longer muzzles, and they were not as wide in front.

When English laws banned blood sports in 1835, the interest in breeding Bulldogs waned, and the breed almost became extinct. The breed was later resurrected, and around the middle of the nineteenth century, Bulldogs appeared in English dog shows. The Bullmastiff is 40 percent Bulldog.

Their great size, strength, and appearance are exemplified by the Mastiff, sometimes erroneously called the Old English Mastiff, a specific breed that is common today in England and the United States. The Bullmastiff is 60 percent Mastiff.

Uses of the Mastiff

The Mastiff has shared British lives and homes for hundreds (or perhaps thousands) of years. A Mastiff is formidable in size and appearance but is quite responsive to handling and training. It was a watchdog that was tied up in yards during the day and let loose when the sun went down. Peasants and royalty alike owned Mastiffs; they were everybody's dogs.

Uses of the Bulldog

The Bulldog got its name from the blood sport called bullbaiting that was very popular in ancient England. Bulldogs were bred for

Each of these cuddly puppies will grow into more than 100 pounds (45 kg) of pure power.

their exceptional courage and persistence in that sport. One big Bulldog tackled the bull by grabbing its ear, and held on tightly. Because of the Bulldog's underbite and massive jaw muscles, it could weigh the bull's head down while a smaller Bulldog grabbed the poor bull by the nose. Together they usually withstood the bull's tossing head, and eventually they pulled him backward and won the contest.

When interest waned in that cruel pastime, the Bulldog was pitted against bears in a similar struggle, and dogfights were staged that ended only when one combatant was dead. In those days Bulldogs were ferocious animals and gutsy to say the least, and some dog fanciers must have recognized that their ferocity was a characteristic that could be subdued through careful selective breeding. Today's Bulldog is the same breed, without the savage traits that made it a tenacious and ferocious fighter.

Guardians of Estates

Why did English landowners decide to use dogs for security? Why not use some other type of defensive measure? Consider the options. To hire an army of men to patrol thousands of acres of thick, dense forest was out of the question.

In those times complex security equipment was unknown. Radio communication, cell phones, and night vision glasses were not yet invented. Motion-operated alarms and cameras were developments of the future. Aircraft or satellite surveillance didn't enter landowners' wildest dreams.

Therefore the landowners used the best they had and put a man and a few dogs in charge

of the estate's security force. Dogs could sniff out poachers that humans would miss and they could move faster than humans in the tangle of forest floors. For those reasons dogs were acceptable candidates for the position of gamekeeper's guardian.

The originators of the Bullmastiff were private regulatory forces who were in charge of the wild game that inhabited the huge forests and estates of the landed gentry. It was the gamekeepers' duty to manage edible wildlife so that it could be harvested by its rightful owners to feed the estates' hundreds of employees.

In short, it was the gamekeepers' responsibility to keep the land free of poachers. Poaching was a capital offense in those days and law enforcement depended upon the felons being delivered alive to the sheriff. Gamekeepers needed the best aides for this important job—athletic, streamlined dogs that were quiet and manageable under all circumstances. Those canine assistants had to be powerful and courageous. They couldn't hesitate to jump on,

He can cover a short distance in seconds, knock down, and hold a poacher for the sheriff.

grip, and hold a poacher for the gamekeeper to transport to the sheriff.

Why were two breeds combined? Why not simply use Mastiffs or Bulldogs? A wonderful guard dog, the Mastiff was a natural choice, but it was too massive and too slow to tackle intruders in the gamekeeper's domain. The Mastiff had been a family pet and protector for many generations and perhaps its aggressiveness had shrunk to fit its domestic role.

The Bulldog was a formidable fighter and would instill fear in would-be poachers by tackling those thoughtless intruders who dared to venture into the woods. However the Bulldog's massive forequarters and head and its relatively short legs rendered it too slow to

pursue and attack a poacher. When a felon was caught, the Bulldog had no trouble overpowering its adversary, but the battle might not stop there. Persistent and resolute, a Bulldog wasn't terribly obedient, and it might maim or kill the interloper before the gamekeeper arrived on the scene. The perfect dog needed to be quiet, agile, and fast enough to catch a running man, knock him down, and keep him down until human help could arrive.

How the Bullmastiff Came to Be

The gamekeepers needed a powerful dog with more athletic ability than either of the progenitor breeds, one that moved quickly and quietly in the thick forest. It had to be a relatively independent, intelligent dog that would act without close handler supervision. It had to be sufficiently trainable to learn to pin a poacher to the ground and guard him until morning when the gamekeeper arrived. They needed a dog with the strength and balance of a Mastiff combined with the spirit and tenacity of a Bulldog. Their goal was a lighter, more streamlined dog than either the Bulldog or the Mastiff.

The colors of the new breed varied between a dark brindle, red, and fawn, and all of the dogs had a dark mask. The brindle is said to have been preferred by gamekeepers because it was more difficult to see at night.

Creating a new breed is not an easy task, and a great deal of closely monitored and selective breeding was needed to eventually produce a breed whose size, conformation, and disposition could be predicted from one generation to the next. Early in the breeding program, consistent conformation and exceptional function were the aims. Gamekeepers knew how they wanted their guardian dogs to look and act.

Many years later the Bullmastiff caught the public's eye and fanciers sought recognition for it from the English Kennel Club. That distinction was awarded when the Bullmastiff bred true to form and function, generation after generation. The new breed's progeny displayed

Official Recognition

The English Kennel Club recognized the Bullmastiff in 1924. The American Kennel Club (AKC) followed suit and recognized the breed in 1933.

TIP

Genetic Makeup

The genetic makeup of the Bullmastiff is 60 percent Mastiff and 40 percent Bulldog.

few of the characteristics of either of the two contributing breeds and presented a phenotype that was distinct from both.

So much for form, but what about function? Twenty-four years before the Bullmastiff was recognized by the English Kennel Club, a famous exhibition was held at a dog show in August of 1901. W. Burton, owner of Thorneywood Kennels of Nottingham, offered a cash prize to anyone who could escape from a muzzled Bullmastiff. One foolhardy but brave spectator volunteered. The Bullmastiff was held while the man ran ahead, and when the dog was released, it overtook, leaped upon, and knocked down the man, holding him until the handler arrived. After several tries, the courageous man gave up and the prize was awarded to the Bullmastiff.

In 1993, the Bullmastiff's standing in the American Kennel Club (AKC) was 62nd place, and only 518 Bullmastiffs were registered that year. Of 151 total breeds listed in 2003 by the AKC, the Bullmastiff was ranked 48th, with 2,943 Bullmastiffs registered. The first American Bullmastiff, registered in 1934 by the AKC, was named Fascination of Felons Fear, a name that emphasizes the breed's strength and resolution. Bullmastiffs are among the stalwarts of the canine species, known for their toughness, tenacity, and courage.

PREPARATION FOR A BULLMASTIFF PUPPY

Proper preparation for any important event in your life is critical to ensure its success. A number of factors are unique to preparing for a live addition to your household, not the least of which is thoughtful consideration of the lifestyle you lead. Equally important is the quality of life you can offer your peerless new pet.

What Is a Bullmastiff?

A Bullmastiff is among the strongest dogs alive—never a vicious dog, but one that obeys its owner's commands with adequate training. It descended from a guard dog, a patrol dog, a dog that was bred specifically to chase down and attack human beings. The modern Bullmastiff has retained its phenotype, yet it has evolved from very specific guarding duties into the role of an excellent family pet. However, an owner must never forget this dog's beginning.

Today's Bullmastiff is a complete companion, but it does not meet every family's needs because of its massive proportions and its general personality. It has great size and powerful musculature, graceful beauty, and alertness. Its

Bullmastiff leadership training and socialization must begin at a very early age.

affectionate demeanor and gentle, inquisitive expression are added to a quiet and rather undemanding attitude. A typical Bullmastiff is a happy and playful dog that is devoted to its family, but it retains the determined guard dog personality of its ancestors. *It can be aggressive with strangers, children, and other dogs.* Never leave your Bullmastiff off-lead or unattended in any area where it may encounter other people or animals. Study the personality

Names

One of your very first acts after taking your Bullmastiff home will be to give it a name. To eliminate any trace of sexism, two names for our hero and heroine have been chosen. Bard is an old Celtic word that referred to a strolling minstrel. Vicki is short for Victoria, a famous queen of England.

traits that accompany the breed before you go any further in your search for a Bullmastiff.

Needs vs. Resources

You know you want a dog, particularly a big dog. But why not one of the dozens of other big dog breeds? Maybe you fancy a big, self-confident dog that is ready to please, trainable, and mild mannered, one that is trustworthy and good natured. Now your motive for acquiring a Bullmastiff becomes clearer.

Any member of the canine species will make significant demands on your time and wallet. Vicki will grow up to be a huge housedog. She needs family interaction and will wither on the vine if kept in a pen or left to her own devices in a lonely backyard.

She needs the best food available and plenty of it; however, she is prone to obesity if the quality and quantity of her meals aren't closely monitored. Her exercise needs are nominal; in fact, she should not be encouraged to exercise strenuously or excessively during her growing phase. As an adult she will appreciate outings but isn't a great jogging companion. A romp in the backyard or a couple of daily walks on a leash will suffice for your Bullmastiff.

She will be quite patient with children, but without training she can show dominant characteristics and can be grouchy with other pets. Vicki must receive a large helping of canine socialization training while still a puppy to curb her potential for aggressiveness toward other dogs. She will greet and socialize with your family's friends and guests after they are properly introduced, but strangers are usually stopped in their tracks when they approach Vicki's home. She requires an authoritative trainer who uses gentle consistency and fairness. However she will rebel at brutality and doesn't appreciate mindless repetition of simple training exercises. As an adult, Vicki will be tough and powerful, but as a puppy, her weight, body mass, and clumsiness can present problems when young children are allowed to handle her without supervision.

Can You Afford a Bullmastiff?

Originally Bullmastiffs were kept only by a few rich British landowners, but today many families in the United States have sufficient funds to buy the pet of their choice. Remember, though, that *afford* is a paradoxical word—having the money for Vicki's initial purchase isn't the whole answer. *A more pertinent condition is whether you possess sufficient knowledge of and dedication to a Bullmastiff.*

Money

As the saying goes, it's your money! However, before you start saving your pennies or enter a line item on your budget, you should look closely at how your money will follow a pricey Bullmastiff.

Consider the size of the adult *Bullmastiff when you buy dishes, collars, and leashes.*

Vicki's purchase price will be significant. Price mostly depends upon supply and demand, but unfortunately for prospective owners, the supply of well-bred Bullmastiff puppies typically equals the demand. Reputable Bullmastiff breeders aren't found around every corner, and most of them aren't in the business to get rich. However, if you want an admirable Bullmastiff puppy, you will pay in excess of $1,000. The costs of breeding and raising a litter of good Bullmastiff puppies are staggering. Puppy prices depend on whether you want a fine representative of the breed or will settle for something less. Talk to owners and breeders at local dog shows about the price you can expect to pay for a puppy—you'll get a lot of other advice from those fanciers at the same time.

You must also consider the cost of the food and services Vicki will need. Visit a pet supply store and price the premium brands of dog food. Read the labels carefully to find out approximately how much food she will need each month. Remember, she will probably reach 100 lbs. (45 kg) or more at maturity.

Check the cost of equipment such as large stainless steel dishes and a platform to hold them steady. Ask your veterinarian if you need a stand to raise food and water dishes off the floor to the proper height for a giant adult. You will probably need a buckle collar and a chain training collar as well as leashes of various types. Check into a head halter and ask about the types available and their use.

Visit local animal hospitals and talk to a veterinary technician about the cost of routine

procedures such as puppy vaccinations, boosters, and parasite control products (don't forget heartworm, flea, and tick preparations). The same technician can probably tell you the cost of the routine maintenance visits that are necessary to properly raise your giant companion. If you intend to show or breed Vicki, you must have her hips and elbows X-rayed at about two years of age and her eyes examined by a veterinary ophthalmologist.

The Bullmastiff is a gentle, intelligent companion that thrives on training.

Your backyard must be fenced if it is not already. A smaller pen and kennel might be included on your checklist, but you shouldn't plan to keep a Bullmastiff in a pen except under particular, limited circumstances.

You may need your breeder's advice and perhaps a professional trainer's help to control her potential for aggressiveness toward other dogs, or in some cases, toward humans. Group training, puppy kindergarten, and obedience classes are important considerations with significant costs.

Add up your figures to calculate a rough annual cost, but always expect the unexpected.

Time

Your time is the most important personal cost to you, and Vicki needs a lot of it. Personal time is all too frequently omitted in planning for dog ownership. Don't underestimate the hours you will need to spend with your companion—if you can't spare at least a half hour to an hour each and every day to play with and exercise her, train, groom, and talk to her, better buy a goldfish instead. Ask a breeder or an owner of a mannerly and contented Bull-mastiff how much one-on-one time they spend with their dogs, and don't assume that you can reduce that time to suit yourself or to fit into your lifestyle. Be ready to compromise and to give up some of your present activities to make room for Vicki's needs.

Home

Your home will also be Vicki's home. She must come and go in your house, and it must be a clean and comfortable place to live. You can be sure she will track grass or mud onto your tile and rugs. She will shed on the furniture that she rubs against. Her tail is like a magic wand; one wave of that sturdy appendage and knickknacks disappear from the coffee table, some never to be found.

All puppies learn about their environment by tasting, mouthing, and chewing. It won't take long to train Vicki to chew her own toys, but consider the damage she may cause to shoes and furniture during the puppyhood training period. Another compromise may require your family to become neater in their habits by picking up and putting away personal items in a secure place. A Bullmastiff isn't a tidy eater so her feeding place must be carefully chosen. Some of these big dogs are droolers, which can be another housekeeping challenge.

Neighbors

Neighbors should be alerted to your planned purchase before you buy a Bullmastiff. Discuss Vicki's breed in general, her adult size, temperament, and gentle disposition. Tell them about the volume of a Bullmastiff's voice, but be sure to add that most aren't problem barkers. Tell your friends and neighbors about a Bullmastiff's protective nature. Take interested neighbors to a local dog show and let them see for themselves just what your dog will look

TIP

Guard Against Boredom
A bored Bullmastiff is an insecure dog that will become timid, noisy, and melancholy if left alone for extended periods.

like and how she will act as an adult. Usually, conscientious owners and breeders will be happy to talk about their dogs to anyone who will listen, and that discussion will do more to inform your neighbors about Bullmastiffs than any book.

As soon as Vicki is comfortable in your home and vaccinated against puppyhood diseases, invite your neighbors in for a backyard barbeque and introduce her to them. Support that experience by furnishing a small handful of nutritious, low-calorie treats for the visitors to feed her. Continue the public relations efforts and frequently invite your closest neighbors and friends, including their children, into your home. Vicki will soon recognize them at first sight. By the time she is fully grown, she will accept your friends and, equally important, your friends will accept her for what she is: a beautiful, extra-large dog that is totally trustworthy around her friends and family.

Insurance

Check your homeowner's policy for pet riders and if you find one, speak to your agent about the wording. Many agents don't know a Rottweiler from a Pomeranian, but they will shudder when they hear you are buying a Bullmastiff. The term *bull* suggests a relation-

—— TIP ——

Getting Help

If at any time Vicki shows any aggressive tendencies toward other dogs or humans, you should ask for professional help immediately. Don't hesitate to ask your veterinarian, Vicki's breeder, or an experienced trainer for advice and assistance. It is critical to stop that vice before it causes a serious problem. Group training, puppy kindergarten, and obedience classes also are important considerations, and significant costs are attached to any professional training.

ship to a pit fighter and conveys fears of vicious dogs that are frequently reported in newspapers. Inform your agent of the Bullmastiff's gentle nature. Explain Vicki's personality and attitude and assure him that you aren't training an attack dog or buying a vicious animal from an inappropriate source.

Dealing with Growth

A Bullmastiff's rapid growth rate can be problematic and a great deal must be learned about big dogs' development before you embark on Bullmastiff ownership. Generally, big dogs gain weight faster but reach maturity later than smaller breeds. Vicki needs as much—or more—attention, love, and handling as a small dog. However, she requires a slightly different approach.

Get down on the floor to pet her. Don't put her on your lap when seated in a chair. Discourage her from jumping up; when you return home and she wants to greet you, sit on the floor and allow her to climb on your lap. She will lick your chin as quickly and as lovingly as any little dog and will appreciate all the time you spend with her on her level.

Lifting the Dog

Discourage children from picking up your puppy because, if dropped, even from a short distance, she may suffer a bone fracture. If she begins to fall and is caught by a leg, her heavy body may stress and tear ligaments and tendons, which may result in permanent lameness, not to mention significant scars on your bank account. Adults and children alike should always interact with Vicki at her level on the floor. There will be times when you must pick her up, but you should minimize that weight-lifting process! Sleeping on your bed is a no-no because of the height. These rules of conduct are a part of owning and loving a Bullmastiff and neglecting them may be painful for both you and Vicki.

Exercise

Too much exercise too soon can be highly detrimental to a fast-growing Bullmastiff's health because of her heavy body mass. Vicki needs close monitoring and *limited* exercise. Don't let her rugged appearance and tough attitude fool you. A Bullmastiff puppy's weight is not balanced with the immaturity of her joint structures. To maximize the positive effects of exercise, provide exercise periods frequently during the day, both inside the house and in your fenced yard, but be sure that Vicki takes a rest in between. Never allow her to engage in long runs or force her to exercise.

The Bullmastiff is a classically beautiful companion that owners must constantly train.

Use discretion; protect her developing bones and joints; limit the duration and the type of exercise; repeat simple, short exercise sessions frequently. Check with your veterinarian or ask Vicki's breeder before you start a different type of play or increase her exercise time. Failure to consider these factors may adversely affect her health and the cost of ownership.

Timing Is Everything

Don't bring Vicki home to the chaotic confusion of holiday traffic and dozens of children and adults filling the house. Crowds of people will bewilder the new puppy and cause her to be unsure of her place in the family. In-laws and second cousins haven't been taught about Vicki's limitations and their errors in judgment may precipitate serious problems. Food and sweets are plentiful at party time, and Vicki is apt to find all sorts of sins to commit without your notice. She may eat cake, cookies, and decorations of all types; balloons, tassels, and ribbons may be swallowed. Children's rough-housing and playing are difficult to control without hurting their feelings. Don't take a chance with Vicki's health. Leave her at the breeder's until a calm, quiet time.

Bonding

Pick a time to collect Vicki when you will have several days or even a couple of weeks at home. Devote that time to bonding with your new puppy. Brushing, petting, handling, and talking to Vicki are good ways to encourage a tight bond between you that will never be breached. During her first days in your home, you and your family should spend as much time with her as possible. Vicki will quickly learn the pecking order in the household, so be sure that her place is behind those of the human members! You can read more about leadership on pages 46–47.

Infants and Toddlers

Some of the most painful home accidents involve children and puppies. An unsupervised,

Friends and neighbors should be introduced to your Bullmastiff on walks and in your yard.

uninformed child cuddles with a roly-poly puppy and inadvertently steps on, rolls on, or drops the puppy and injures it. That unfortunate event lives in the child's mind for years and the effects on the puppy may be seen even longer. These problems can be avoided with proper training of the adults and children in your household, but teaching requires your time and effort.

Sources of a Good Bullmastiff

Internet advertising presents a scary, ever-expanding source of puppies. Buying a dog from a photograph is not wise. Just because purebred Bullmastiffs are advertised on the Internet doesn't mean that the ads are factual. Until the advertisers' credentials are proven, you might just as well be buying your new puppy sight unseen! Unless you know the Bullmastiff breed and the breeder or have a mentor to advise you, and you see the Bullmastiff puppy with its dam and its siblings, you are asking for trouble. You need to handle the puppy, its siblings, and its mother. You must see the surroundings in which it was raised. You need to examine the dam and sire's pedigree and registration papers, proof of normal hips, elbows, and eyes, and talk to the breeder. Only then should you sign a purchase contract.

Selecting a Reputable Breeder

Selecting a breeder is an excellent time to use the Internet. Go on-line and enter "Ameri-

Lift and hold your Bullmastiff puppy securely to prevent serious injury from falling.

can Bullmastiff Association Inc." in the address line. In a couple of seconds you will see a number of personal ads offering puppies, but they should be ignored because they have nothing to do with the ABA. Somewhere down the page you will find an entry for the AKC Parent Breed Club with the ABA secretary's name and address. Contact that person and ask to receive the names of reputable breeders in your area who are members of the ABA and who can be contacted for information about available litters. Also ask to receive a list of all-breed and specialty dog shows in your area. A specialty show is one in which only one breed or a small number of similar breeds are shown. You are now armed with a list of reputable contacts, and puppy shopping can begin.

Pets vs. Show Dogs

You must decide if you are interested in a show dog or a companion pet. In the eyes of a novice the differences between siblings may be minor, but if you plan to exhibit your Bullmastiff in conformation shows, a tiny difference can be significant. When you contact breeders in your area, let them know that you are seeking a companion pet or a pup with show and breeding potential.

Breeding dams should have faultless temperaments, have earned championship points in the show ring, and have been examined and proven free from hereditary diseases. Superior bitches are bred to males of similar quality, and those matings produce litters of Bullmastiff

puppies that aren't necessarily showstoppers but that meet the breed standard. A breeder may keep a puppy or two from a litter to show and offer the remaining puppies for sale. Occasionally a winning show dog will emerge from a Bullmastiff puppy that was sold as a pet, but that Cinderella story is rare.

Show and breeding Bullmastiff puppies may be priced a bit higher than pet-quality littermates, or their prices may be equal. Littermates all have the same genetic background; their appearance and heredity give them every chance to become fine companion pets. Buying a breeding or show potential puppy does not increase the value of your pet. Far more important is Vicki's personality and temperament,

Breeders typically screen new owners before placing their puppies.

which are enhanced by nurturing from wean-ing-time onward. Her disposition depends on your ability to properly socialize her, your time spent with her bonding and training, your feeding and handling techniques, and of course the health care she is given.

Breeders' Questions

Once you have located a couple of breeders, you should visit their facilities and meet some of their breeding stock. A reputable breeder usually does not have dozens off Bullmastiffs to choose from, and the dog kennel is run from the family home. Good Bullmastiff breeding is a fancier's sideline, with perhaps a couple of show dogs that are part-time breeding bitches. Maybe the home will include a male that is being cam-paigned on the show circuit and a puppy or two that are likely show prospects. The breeder may proudly show you some fine Bullmastiff pictures and maybe give you a tour of the house, where you'll see prize ribbons everywhere.

When you begin talking puppies, the breeder will ask you dozens of questions. He may ask how you learned of the breed. He will ask about the ages of children in your family, the size of your house, the type of fence around the backyard, and whether or not you have previous experience with big dogs. If you answer yes to that question, he may ask if your prior experience was satisfactory or if you were disappointed with the big dog. He will undoubtedly ask if you plan to have the puppy neutered, and if not, why. He may ask if you are aware of the short life of many Bullmastiffs. He may quiz you about the nature of your work, your hours, and how much time you and other adults of the household will have to devote to the care of the puppy. He will want to know if your budget for the puppy will be sufficient to allow for good nutrition and professional health care. He may ask if you know how to socialize the puppy and if you know of a good training class near you. If the breeder doesn't receive the answers he wants, he will probably end the conversation and the prospective sale.

Preferred Gender

Deciding on puppy gender is mostly personal preference. Some Bullmastiff males can be aggressive toward strange dogs, and they don't lose all of that aggressiveness after being neutered. However, most neutered males and spayed females are less aggressive, and either sex will be a fantastic pet if given a chance. In a household with a male and female, the female usually will dominate the male. Female puppies are thought by some breeders to be more focused, more trainable, and quicker to learn than males. If you are like many novices and the Bullmastiff is your first giant breed, you should discuss the question of gender with the breeder and take his advice.

Choosing Your Puppy

You've done your homework and located some reputable breeders in your area. You've seen their breeding stock and asked one breeder to call you when his pregnant bitch whelps. You saw the puppies at four weeks of age and fell in love with the whole litter. At eight weeks they've been weaned, received their first vaccination, and you have an appointment to see the puppies again. You've been advised that all the puppies will be sold as companion pets and you are anxious to see them and choose one.

The breeder will probably point out certain puppies that are more or less aggressive than others, some that may be mischief-makers, and others that are more timid. He might tell you the shier puppies will not be ready for adoption

CHECKLIST

Selection Strategies

✔ Sit quietly on the floor, hands at your sides, saying nothing. The better socialized puppies will probably climb all over you.

✔ Pay close attention to the puppy who licks your fingers, nibbles your chin, and climbs on and off your lap fearlessly.

✔ Ask the breeder to take that puppy into another room where you can continue. Sit beside the puppy on the floor with your legs outstretched, arms at your sides.

✔ Talk to her and reassure her, but don't reach for her. Let her make the first move.

✔ She will probably climb on your lap and try to reach your face with her speedy tongue. Don't pull back. She won't understand that you have accepted her as a friend if you deny her face-licking.

✔ Lie on the floor beside her and continue quietly talking to her.

✔ Without hurrying, rub her neck gently, lift her ears, and lightly scratch under her chin.

✔ After a few minutes slowly turn her on her side while you continue petting her. When she relaxes, carefully turn her upside down and rub her tummy and legs briefly before letting her go.

If she doesn't resist your caresses and trusts your hands and voice, the puppy is probably an excellent choice. If she zips back on your lap when you sit up and follows your footsteps when you stand and walk toward the door, you know she is the one and bonding has already begun!

as soon as others, but a slightly bashful puppy may behave differently when it is taken away from its siblings. He may speak of minor marking or conformation differences and explain the significance of each. He probably will tell you that mischievous puppies are often more active and will be easier to train than those who display more reticent attitudes. Listen carefully to the breeder's comments and don't hesitate to ask questions about the meaning of puppy behavior.

Canine psychologists and some breeders perform personality testing. The results of those tests may be disputed because an individual can be attracted to a particular puppy's personality and some puppies choose one certain person to love more than others. You *do* need instruction in interpreting puppy behavior, but you can probably choose your companion puppy without professional analysis.

Health Guarantees

Choosing your canine companion is secondary only to choosing your spouse. Many professional Bullmastiff breeders will guarantee the health of their puppies if the buyer takes the puppy directly from their premises to a veterinarian for examination. If the veterinarian detects any illness or signs of an impending disease, the puppy will be reclaimed by the breeder and a full refund will be given to the buyer. However, only an inexperienced amateur breeder will guarantee a puppy's good health for a period of time that extends more than a day or two after she is taken to your home. The reasons for that should be quite obvious, but in case they aren't, consider the mistakes that can be made when a new puppy goes to a new home surrounded by new people, new events,

and no telling how many physical hazards. The possible pitfalls are too numerous to mention.

On the brighter side, many breeders will guarantee their puppies' *genetic* health for life and will replace a Bullmastiff that proves to be hereditarily crippled no matter when the disease strikes. Such a guarantee usually does not include full refund of your purchase price but it might provide a new dog of equal quality from the breeder's next litter. Unfortunately, that guarantee doesn't address the time you've spent with your pet or the affection you've received from and given to the sick companion. It can't possibly erase the disappointment or expenses you encounter when your Bullmastiff suffers a protracted genetic illness or must be euthanized. The most important point to remember: Try very hard to make the right selection the first time around.

Another guarantee a breeder should make is to take back your Bullmastiff if it proves to be more dog than you can handle, if its temperament is faulty, or if for any reason you simply can't keep the dog. Be sure to receive a full explanation and get the guarantees in writing.

Puppy Needs vs. Young Adult Needs

If you aren't sure you can adequately raise and train a puppy for any reason, consider adopting an adult. An older dog may reduce your total cash outlay, and the time necessary for training might be much less. If you are buying from a reputable breeder, you know the dog's nutrition has been excellent. The dog has been raised by professionals, whose experience should assure you that it has received proper handling, socialization, and training.

Adult Bullmastiffs, especially young dogs that have not been mishandled or abused, will bond quickly with another family. Those dogs

Before choosing a puppy, check the dam, sire, and others from the bloodline if possible.

are good natured, even tempered, and will appreciate the quiet gentleness that you offer. The bond between you and your companion will grow from the first day onward and will become as strong as if it had been established at an early age. Check out these options:

• Many breeders keep a puppy or two to exhibit in conformation shows, and some of those puppies are less-than-perfect show dogs when they mature. They are fine Bullmastiff specimens, but they just can't compete favorably with the quality of dogs in the show ring. Consequently, as young adults, they are available for adoption. The price for those dogs may be less than for weanling puppies, but the advantages are many. They have already received immunizations and have been checked for parasites. In addition, they have been housebroken and leash trained.

• Sometimes a throwback puppy with a deformed tail or incorrect mask or color shows up in a litter of Bullmastiffs. The breeder may not find it a proper home for several months and may be in a mood to negotiate the price.

• Contact the ABA and ask if rescue dogs are available.

Rescued Adults

Bullmastiff rescue organizations, which are run by conscientious breeders and fanciers, are found in every region of the country. A rescue is a volunteer group that houses and cares for Bullmastiffs that find themselves in shelters or

A quiet dam often produces very trainable puppies.

zations may have waiting lists for their dogs, but if you are interested, their names and addresses can be found on the ABA's Internet Web page. Rescued dogs often lack canine and human social skills, some have been mistreated, some lack good manners, and a few bitches have been overbred, but they can make excellent pets with your patience and persistence.

What Is a Backyard Breeder?

A backyard breeder is an amateur dog breeder with very little knowledge and questionable motives. Reputable Bullmastiff breeders rarely place newspaper advertisements. Want ads are the tools of backyard breeders and an occasional owner who must give up a pet and hasn't heard of rescue organizations. A typical backyard breeder will acquire a female Bullmastiff puppy from any source, usually from another backyard breeder. That greedy individual proposes to recoup the price of his pet by breeding the bitch at the earliest opportunity, selling the puppies to anyone who will buy them and getting rich in the process. He finds a mercenary partner who has a male Bullmastiff and the pair agree to breed the bitch to the male without regard for conformational or personality problems either parent may exhibit. Obviously, their program is fraught with financial difficulties. General health or hereditary soundness does not enter the equation. After a few puppies are born with deformities or foul dispositions, the bitch may be retired or spayed, but the damage to the breed is done and the buyers of the puppies will have paid the price for their ignorance.

pounds. A rescue will also take abused dogs, injured dogs, and homeless pets that are found on the streets. Many rescued Bullmastiffs were wonderful pets, and all are worthy of a second chance. While they are kept by the rescue organization, their wounds are healed and their temperaments are calmed as much as possible.

Before being offered for adoption, each rescued dog is examined for health, temperament tested, vaccinated, neutered or spayed, examined for parasites, and put on a preventive health program. Its nutrition also is brought up to standard. A nominal fee is charged to offset some of the expenses incurred in health care and housing. Rescued dogs are placed only in homes where they will receive the finest care and attention. In the event that a rescued dog doesn't work out, it will be reclaimed by the rescue organization. Bullmastiff rescue organi-

Be sure your Bullmastiff will accept another dog before you attempt to exercise them together.

Puppy Mills

Probably the only source of puppies that is worse than a backyard breeder is a puppy mill—a disreputable dog breeder who mass-produces puppies from bitches obtained from pounds and newspaper ads. The proprietors of these kennels cut corners at every opportunity, as their only goal is to produce *purebred* puppies as cheaply as possible. Their businesses thrive on the plentiful numbers of uninformed buyers, vaccination shortcuts, and a disregard for their breeding stock's general and hereditary health, nutrition, and hygiene. These individuals usually maintain their operations on the outskirts of good-size cities in housing that is unencumbered by zoning laws and neighborhood restrictions. They unload their pitiful puppies on uninformed citizens through newspaper ads, and all too frequently they sell those puppies wholesale to pet dealers in nearby cities.

Bullmastiffs aren't as popular as small breeds in a puppy mill for several reasons.
✔ They are frequently problem breeders.
✔ Often they are delivered by cesarean section.
✔ Litter size is comparatively small.
✔ Cost of food is quite high.
✔ Lives are relatively short.

Raising a Bullmastiff is not a highly specialized or complicated endeavor if you are careful not to make too many errors. Mistakes usually are caused by not understanding your dog's needs, and the primary thing that he needs is you!

Puppy Behavior

Dogs retain a few wolflike genetic characteristics from their ancestors. Bard's behavior is deeply ingrained in his genetics and is sometimes difficult or impossible to change. Certain Bullmastiff behaviors are relatively fixed because of many generations of selective breeding, but they remain somewhat malleable. Still other habits stem from personal experiences and are uniquely Bard's. These more recently learned behaviors can be readily modified.

Bard has some characteristics of Bullmastiffs living in the nineteenth century, but remember that he is many generations removed from those dogs; his more recent experiences also influence his behavior. He is a keen, intelligent, thinking companion. His first response to any situation might be what you would expect from an early-day Bullmastiff, not what you

Proper training and handling will lead to trust, obedience, and a well-socialized companion.

expect of your companion. Don't despair! You can modify that inappropriate response with proper training and gentle handling. He can be taught to respond quickly and appropriately to new situations by using his reasoning faculties to solve problems. Positive experience is gained every day, and Bard's intelligence increases with each problem he encounters and subsequently solves. As an adult his behavior and personality will be as distinctive as his bark. *You are Bard's alter ego; you have the opportunity to shape many of his habits and personality characteristics to your design.*

Negative communication and lack of communication are major mistakes that can ruin your efforts. Watch Bard's body language and facial expressions closely. He will reveal things about himself that will enhance communication and understanding between the two of you, making training easier.

Bard is also interested in learning about *your* quirks and idiosyncrasies, and your habits will influence his learning. By speaking to him qui-

After he is leash-trained, the retractable leash is used to allow your Bullmastiff more freedom.

etly and distinctly, he will learn to expect that tone and will respond to you much more quickly than if you raise your voice.

If you expect Bard to respond to situations appropriately at all times, be sure that your response to his conduct is always appropriate. Reward his desirable behavior with quick praise and gentle touch. Dismiss unacceptable conduct with a quick, sharp *no* spoken in a normal voice. Then move on and ignore the negative behavior as if it never happened.

Treat Bard's behavioral idiosyncrasies quickly but considerately. Don't overrespond to an undesirable action with a long tirade of scold-

ing. Nagging will give him the impression that his undesirable action was an important event that should be remembered, and he may repeat it just to see if you recollect your speech. By the same token, if you overrespond to a desirable habit with great applause, lengthy praise, and lots of tidbits, he may repeat the event each time he wants a treat. Aim for a happy medium.

Natural Urges

Urination and Defecation

Canines typically want to urinate and defecate away from their dens. Depositing his body wastes away from the nest is a hereditary trait that Bard will practice when possible. Therefore, if you want to promote house training, don't make the mistake of scolding or reprimanding Bard for doing what comes naturally, no matter where he does it. You should take him to his toilet area as often as he needs to go. Remember that, as a puppy, he will have that need at least half a dozen times every day.

Licking

You may have observed Bard's siblings licking their dam's face as well as each other's faces. Think back: What are the first things he wanted to share with you? His busy tongue and his wagging tail! His wag tells you "We're friends." He wants you to kneel down so he can greet you properly. He can't pucker, so his wet tongue is the closest thing to a kiss that he can manage. Licking and wagging are lifelong canine traits.

Watch your dog carefully when you allow sniffing.

Bard will probably take a fancy to toddlers in your family if they are taught not to pick him up. Interaction between young children and puppies is natural because the child offers a face that is within reach and most children won't resist a puppy's wet kisses. Of course a trace of milk, candy, or peanut butter is the icing on the cake. It often seems that a puppy would like his master to reciprocate and lick his face. Although Bard would consider himself a really important member of the family if the leader of the pack licked his puppy face, at least allow him to take a few licks on your chin before you stand up. He will appreciate your understanding and will probably repeat the action the next time you meet. It is a serious mistake to discourage that natural greeting.

Mouthing

Mouthing is another natural or genetic behavior of all canines. Bard wants to taste everything in his environment so he will remember it the next time he meets it. You can't change his mouthing habit but you can channel his behavior to appropriate targets. Unfortunately, *excessive* mouthing leads to chewing, which changes the shape and character of the items being chewed, resulting in angry people. Don't make the mistake of displaying your wrath when you find your brand-new alligator belt all slimy and gnarled with a new set of holes. If your first impulse is to use that chewed-up scrap to teach your Bullmastiff a lesson he'll never forget, first consider his perspective:

A brindle Bullmastiff focuses on his owner for instruction.

1. He saw the belt as just another piece of sweet-tasting leather.

2. He didn't chew the belt maliciously.

3. He forgot the event promptly.

4. He won't be remorseful no matter what you do.

If you make a big deal out of the event, he will be confused and upset, and the experience will teach him a few things about you:

1. Your actions are unpredictable.

2. You yelled and screamed and scolded him when you came in the room.

3. You threatened or hit him cruelly.

4. You can't be trusted.

A threat of abuse is just another form of abuse. When you act out of your usual character, you will defeat hours—even weeks or months—of bonding. Remember:

1. Your actions mold the personality of your valued and loving friend.

2. You left the belt hanging over a chair where it was quite accessible to your companion.

3. You are older, smarter, and more intelligent than Bard and should have known better than to place a tasty new object in his path.

Don't be discouraged, but do take responsibility for your actions. Pick up the belt and hang it in the closet in plain view to remind you of your mistake. Then forget the incident.

Jumping Up

Jumping up is merely a way for puppy Bard to reach your face to employ his official face-licking greeting. He doesn't mean to snag your socks or scratch your ankles. Jumping up is cute

A well-trained Bullmastiff can be handled by almost any family member.

when he is tiny, but the behavior is no longer cute when he weighs more than a hundred pounds and jumps up on an unsuspecting petite visitor. It's a mistake to allow that bad habit to get started. Unless he is taught otherwise, he doesn't even consider jumping up as inappropriate behavior. You must instruct him, quietly and consistently, and at the same time substitute a more socially acceptable action. Don't overreact! Modify the behavior, but not with anger.

On his first day in your household, when he jumps up, back up quickly and say *"Bard, sit!"* Then kneel down to his level, speak gently, and pet him. After his wet greeting is expressed on your chin, stand and turn away.

Another highly effective technique can be used when he is less than three months old. It requires a couple of young children to take part. Explain to the children their roles in the play before you bring Bard into the act, then call your Bullmastiff from the house. He will see his playmates, run to them, and jump up on his favorite child. Immediately that child pretends to be hurt, topples over backward, and pretends to cry. Moaning and crying loudly, the child rises, turns, slowly limps away, and disappears into the house. During the theatrics, the child actor doesn't speak to Bard and totally ignores him. Watch the effect on your companion and repeat the act with several children over the

A Bullmastiff has a good appetite and should not be fed table scraps.

Diet Changes

Owners who want the very best food for their Bullmastiff often make the major mistake of changing his diet too quickly. *Diet changes are dangerous for a young puppy* because they can cause an upset stomach and precipitate diarrhea, vomiting, and loss of control. These problems may interfere with nutritional balance and housebreaking. When you pick up Bard from the breeder, ask for a small bag of his ration. Buy more of the same food and don't even think of changing his diet for at least a week or more. If you feel it necessary to change his diet, do so after Bard has acclimated to your household and become accustomed to your hours and feeding times. Then, if you have read or heard of a better, more nutritious ration, buy some and add it to his existing ration little by little until a complete conversion has been made.

next few days. The results will amaze you. That bit of acting should be used only when Bard weighs less than twenty-five pounds.

Sleeping Accommodations

Where does Bard sleep? Ideally a puppy should sleep in your bedroom where you can hear him and take him out when he becomes restless during the night. His quarters might be a very large fiberglass shipping crate or an exercise pen of modest dimensions. Add his blanket or pad and put him to bed with a couple of chewies, such as pressed rawhide or nylon bones, to keep him busy. Avoid the mistake of allowing him to sleep on your bed. New habits are quickly learned, and if he is ever allowed on your bed it will be very difficult to change that behavior.

Puppy-Proofing Your Home

A Bullmastiff puppy left alone is a disaster looking for a place to happen. Bard doesn't plan it that way, but he may become a tremendous problem if left to his own devices. He wants to investigate everything in his environment; he is born with a curiosity to find out how everything works and the willingness to eat anything that doesn't attack him. Those inherent traits can be his undoing.

Neglect Leads to Disaster

You and your knowledge are Bard's greatest needs while he is being raised and are necessary to produce a fine companion. Arrange the hours in your day to accommodate Bard's needs. In some situations you can delegate caring for his

CHECKLIST

Necessary Safety Precautions

Indoors

✔ Kitchen: Never leave food within range of Bard's tongue. Secure bottom cupboards and trash containers from puppy invasion, and never leave cleaning chemicals within his reach.

✔ Home office: Make sure computer and telephone cords are secured out of reach. If books are kept on exposed shelves, move them to higher, inaccessible shelves.

✔ Bedroom: Don't leave clothes, shoes, or belts lying on chairs or under the bed. Keep closet doors closed. Secure lamp cords out of Bard's reach.

✔ Empty wastebaskets regularly and don't toss interesting items into them that might be chewed or swallowed.

✔ Living room: Secure all television and lamp cords from Bard's reach. Put away any tasseled rugs until he is older. Keep all edibles off coffee tables and end tables.

✔ Dining room: Don't use tablecloths that hang invitingly over the sides of the table.

✔ Be sure Bard is in another room when food is served and never, ever give him tidbits from the table.

✔ Bathrooms: Keep the toilet lid down all the time. Empty wastebaskets daily or keep them inside a closed cabinet.

✔ Laundry room: Keep all soaps and laundry products on the upper shelves or inside closed cupboards. Brooms and mops should be hung out of Bard's reach. Exposed washer and dryer hoses and cords should be secured out of his reach. Don't leave an ironing board set up with an iron on it.

✔ Basement: Keep the basement door closed and don't allow Bard to venture down the stairs. Basement storage rooms are the devil's playground. Don't tempt Bard or invite him to enter.

Outdoors

✔ Roll up all water hoses and store them out of reach.

✔ Lock your garden shed and put all insecticides, herbicides, and fertilizers out of reach.

✔ Check the fence for any openings or holes. Make sure that no part of the fence is pulled up from the ground.

✔ Padlock the gate(s) and give the key or combinations only to trusted family members.

physical needs to a family member, but you, the primary owner-handler, are ultimately culpable for any mistakes made in his upbringing. This is a huge responsibility fraught with all sorts of hidden dangers. Mistakes of omission and commission and blunders of every type can crop up, but usually they aren't irreparable. If you just keep your cool and look for good advice, you and Bard will both be winners. Read all you can find about raising a Bullmastiff, separate good advice from bad, and put to use all the good ideas you find.

TRAINING

Many types of training are discussed but one is purposefully omitted. Do not train your Bullmastiff to guard. Never encourage him when he bristles up as a stranger approaches. Discourage his stiff-legged march when another dog comes near. His guarding instinct is deeply ingrained and needs no encouragement!

Why Train?

A happy Bullmastiff owner is one who has a well-disciplined, beautifully mannered companion. A big, happy, clumsy puppy will win your heart, but training is required to appreciate Bard when he is a huge adult and his antics are no longer clumsy or cute. In a year or so the roly-poly little mischief-maker with a happy attitude will reach more than one hundred pounds of muscle; he will be powerful and agile enough to wreak havoc if he isn't taught otherwise.

Now and every day is the time to train him with loving kindness, consistency, and a positive

Adequate and continual training is a must for Bullmastiffs.

attitude. Don't allow Bard to become a bully, but don't attempt to eliminate his natural dominance overnight. He always needs security: a backyard fence, a firm hand on his leash, total understanding, and training.

When to Begin

Begin training the day Bard arrives in your home. The professional breeder has given you a head start on developing your Bullmastiff's social skills. However, you must continue socializing him every day with other puppies, friends, and children. Stop a bad habit as soon as it is discovered and replace it with a trait that will be appropriate now and for years to come. Always keep Bard's adult size and physical ability at the front of your mind; although he is now a little puppy, visualize him as an

A pair of Bullmastiff puppies share their space in an exercise pen.

tively bred to hunt down, catch, and hold human poachers. Further back in his family tree are Bulldogs that were specifically bred to fight with other dogs and other animals. Remember that, although inbred influences can be difficult to eliminate, Bullmastiff owners must make a serious, concentrated effort to modify those traits.

Socialization is not a lesson that can be taught one time and then be forgotten; it is an ongoing, never-ending obligation. Every walk in the park and every time friends come to your home, every time you encounter a wheelchair, shopping cart, or bicycle is an opportunity to teach acceptable social behavior.

Bard's socialization must receive your ongoing attention. Remember, however, that your Bullmastiff has many generations of beautifully adjusted and loving family pets in his background. He isn't vicious; he won't arbitrarily seek out people to attack, and he is not likely to become malevolent if his socialization continues throughout life. Strive for total control, but don't expect his attitude to be converted to that of a lapdog.

adult every day. When he is tiny, give him a break; remember his immaturity. His young mind doesn't process complicated material, but as he becomes more able to learn and retain instruction, give him more challenges.

Socialization

Bullmastiffs generally are easy to socialize, but to neglect that aspect of Bard's training is a horrible mistake! *Human* socialization means training Bard to behave in his role as a canine member of a human pack. *Canine* socialization relates to training him to behave around other dogs. In both cases you should remember his heritage. His Bullmastiff ancestors were selec-

Train Yourself

Teaching is a double-edged sword. You must first learn how to superintend proper training. Interactive training classes are invaluable and are available from professional dog trainers that you can contact through your local Bullmastiff club. Thousands of American dogs are euthanized needlessly every year because the owners *thought* they could train their dogs.

Consistency

Plan thoughtfully and teach consistently. Think about what you want Bard to become, then schedule his lessons and teach him accordingly. His inherent intelligence, pleasant puppyhood experiences, and above-average trainability will serve you well, but do not hurry the process. Keep your expectations realistic. No two dogs are identical—you must be flexible but never lose sight of your goals.

First teach him his name, then the most important of all commands, *come*. At the same time begin house training. When he has begun to grasp those fundamentals, teach him *sit, stay, down*, and *halt*. Make your training sessions short, no more than ten minutes a couple of times a day. Teach commands one by one and repeat the lesson a few times in each session until he understands it completely; don't nag him or make him repeat an exercise until he rebels. Evaluate his accomplishments weekly and you will be surprised at his learning rate. Pat yourself on the back when he instantly recognizes and performs each command quickly. Teach other commands that have special meaning such as *off, up, walk on, stand*, and so forth. Slowly add other challenges such as hide and seek, and tracking.

Command Language and Tone

Be consistent with your tone as well as with the words you use. Using your most distinctive, calm voice, tell him crisply, *"Bard, come."* After hearing that tone and those words a few times,

A Bullmastiff must be kept busy with new challenges to stay happy and contented.

TIP

Worth Repeating

Repetitious training is boring! Endless repeating will be rejected after a task is learned!

he will begin to expect them. Before he hears the second word he'll know that a command is on its way and will listen for it very carefully. Do not complicate a command with useless words such as *come here, come over here*. It is futile to speak to him as if he were an adult human. When you tell him sternly, *"Bard, you*

Canine and human socialization are part of any Bullmastiff's training.

stop that and come over here," you will be very fortunate if he understands one word of the eight you've spoken and even more fortunate if he responds to the command.

Very early in training, he will focus on you for hand signals or body English to confirm what he hears. For instance, at the same time you utter "*Come*," wave your hand urging him to come to you. Soon he will look at and focus on you every time he hears his name. Focus is the most important facet of training.

Teaching His Name

Complex names or those that contain more than two syllables are difficult to learn. Bard is a good name. It's easy for everyone to pronounce, quickly spoken, and has a constant

ring to it regardless of how or by whom it is used. When you speak to your Bullmastiff to give him direction—whether or not it is a command or you simply want to get his attention—always use his name first. Say *"Bard, come."* Or *"Bard, sit!"* Or maybe *"Bard, good dog!"*

Crate and Pen Training

Buy a crate large enough for an adult Bullmastiff to stand up comfortably, turn around, and lie down. An extra-large fiberglass shipping crate is expensive but will serve you well. Place inside a soft, easily cleaned blanket and a nylon chewy to teach Bard that the crate is his private, snug refuge, his den, his personal lair. When you crate him don't make a big deal out

Bullmastiffs accept other animals, even Texas Longhorns.

of it. Simply put him in, hand him a small treat, latch the door, and exit. Don't tell him to be good, or that you won't be away long, that you love him, or anything else of that nature. Just leave quickly!

In the beginning, do not leave him inside his crate for more than a few minutes and don't give him another treat or make a fuss over him when you let him out. Build up his crate time very gradually. Remember to reward him for crating and not for de-crating. Within a week, he will go in when you point and tell him *"Crate."*

Bard's crate will protect him from well-meaning but boisterous children when friends come to call. It can be used to transport him safely in your SUV, van, or station wagon. Never use it as a punishment. Never leave him inside for more that an hour at a time except for nighttime sleeping. Leave the crate door open when he is not confined. When he is a puppy, never leave him confined to a crate or pen for longer than four hours unless you like cleaning up messes; puppies do not have sufficient urinary and bowel control to last any longer. As an adult he may be able to spend all night in his crate without incident.

An X-pen is a portable, collapsible, metal barrier that can be used for a number of purposes. Such a pen might serve as Bard's den but probably not for long. Most pens are made to accommodate much smaller dogs and an energetic Bullmastiff puppy will tip one over and walk away. If you use a pen instead of a crate for Bard's confinement, try securing it to a large piece of plywood.

Housebreaking

Housebreaking should be called "owner training" because in order to be quickly and totally successful in that endeavor you must first train yourself and your family. Dogs whose breeders allowed them to leave the whelping nest to deposit their wastes are more easily housebroken.

✔ Upon Bard's arrival at your home, carry him to the toilet area in your backyard, put him down, and remain there until he sniffs and hopefully relieves himself. Only then should you take him into the house.

✔ Return him to that same spot every time you see him acting restlessly, circling, sniffing the floor, looking wistfully at the back door, or whining at the door.

A well-trained Bullmastiff is safe in every situation, even a parade.

✔ Never scold him for having an accident in the house. He wouldn't have messed in the house if you had taken him outside in time.

✔ If you catch him in the act of urination or defecation in the house, pick him up, carry him to the toilet area, and place him on the ground. Then praise him when he is finished. Clean up any mess he left with a cleaner that is designed for that use, *not* an ammonia-based cleaner.

✔ Each time he performs correctly, praise him with a *Good dog!*

✔ Take him to the toilet area immediately after every meal, first thing in the morning,

after he exhibits a burst of energy, and last thing at night.

✔ Pick up his water dish and don't feed him an hour and a half before you retire.

✔ When you put him in his crate for the night, place it near your bed so you can hear him moving about or fussing. Take him to the toilet area and return him directly to the crate. Never play with him, or an aggravating habit will be formed that will be hard to stop.

Collar and Leash

Buckle collars made from leather or nylon webbing are great for Bard to wear when he is lounging around. Rivet his nametag and license on the collar and let him wear it for gradually longer periods until he wears it day and night, except when you are training. Buy one at least several sizes too large because he will grow into and out of it quickly. To measure the correct fit, place two fingers between his neck and the collar and pull it up snuggly.

When Bard is about three or four months old, buy a stainless chain training collar or choke collar. It should be about 2 inches (5.1 cm) greater than the circumference of his neck. Drop the chain through one of the rings to form a noose and snap the leash onto the free ring. Place the collar over his muzzle and on his neck so that the free chain of the collar and leash runs up the left side of his neck and across the top from left to right. When you are walking with him, he should be on your left and the leash should run through your left hand and be held by your right.

When you snug up the collar, the free running chain should exert momentary pressure on his neck, and when you release it, the collar should instantly loosen. This collar should be put on when you are training or taking him out of the yard for a leashed walk. Replace the training collar with his nylon or leather collar when he is loose in the backyard.

If you are of slight build or not as strong as your Bullmastiff, you should try using a head halter. K-9 Cumalong, Halti, BeHave, Gentle Leader, Snoot Loop, or Comfort Halter are good options. Choose the one that fits best and buy it. A harmless piece of control equipment that really works, it will control Bard painlessly and gently. Take Bard to the store with you so a salesperson can show you how to fit the halter properly. When the slack is taken from a leash attached to a head halter, Bard's muzzle will be turned and he will immediately respond by slowing down to slack the leash. If you want more information about the head halter, check your bookstore for Barron's *Dog Training With a Head Halter* by Fields-Babineau. The book will furnish ample advice about training with a head halter.

For training, use a rolled leather, flat leather, nylon, or chain nonexpandable leash about 6 feet long (182 cm). For exercise when you need only minimal control, you can try an expandable leash that retracts when a button is pushed. If you choose a retractable leash, buy the strongest one on the shelf, pair it with a leather or nylon collar, and use it only if your Bullmastiff is already well trained. A retractable leash should only be used for walks in safe areas with no traffic and where you aren't likely to find loose dogs wandering about.

Off-lead exercise is not recommended for Bard any time when he may encounter pedestrians or other dogs. His dormant urges may cost you and your Bullmastiff dearly! Human and canine interaction isn't a great challenge if you have trained him to walk on lead and respond

to *halt* and *sit* commands. However, expect the unexpected and exercise him on a leash!

Introduction to Other Dogs

The easiest time to introduce other dogs is while Bard is still a puppy. Puppies like to play and wrestle with each other and quickly become lifelong friends. Adult dogs will usually accept Bard as a puppy, and he will probably meet and greet each one with an active tongue, curious nose, and wagging tail. He may roll over on his back in submission when approached by an adult. The adult will paw at him, sniff, and turn away, quickly accepting Bard's surrender with gentle gratitude. However, as Bard matures physically and mentally and his hormones change, his agenda may also change, and he may challenge a former friend.

Many dog clubs offer puppy kindergarten classes where you can leave Bard for a number of hours in the company of other young dogs of various breeds. These classes must be well monitored to prevent confrontations and altercations and to be sure that timid dogs contribute to the play and games. Kindergarten is an excellent adjunct to Bard's socialization. Obedience training is also offered by many of the same organizations and is another way to add to Bard's canine socialization. Any kind of closely monitored activities that give him one-on-one contact with other dogs are fine, but don't drop your guard.

Positive Attitude Yields Positive Results

When you encounter another dog on your walks with Bard, never pull him away from the other dog unless you perceive a potential con-

and act positive, but be prepared to take corrective measures.

Training Location

A quiet backyard is perfect for early training. Pick a place where Bard is comfortable and there are no distractions and get his attention by calling his name. Have him sit while you put on his training collar or head halter and leash. Pet and reassure him in a soft-spoken tone before you begin and end each training session. Training should always be a time of bonding, a pleasant time for both of you. If you are in a hurry, better wait until you have more time. If you are in a bad mood, don't expect him to perform as well as when you are happy and at peace with the world. He will perceive your moods from the very first session.

Training Time

Don't spend all afternoon on each session of Bard's schooling. His attention span as a puppy is very limited and his response will diminish if you continually repeat the exercise.

A simple command lesson should take no more than a minute or two and should be repeated twice. The entire session shouldn't last more than ten or fifteen minutes. After he responds quickly to a command, don't nag him or ask for repetition after repetition or you will turn him off. After a while he will do simple tasks quickly and look to you for new challenges. Mental tasks and problem-solving will require more time than simple commands, but his active mind needs problems to resolve.

Training Treats

A tasty treat at the finish of a satisfactory performance should be the norm in almost all

---

═══ TIP ═══

Training

- Never hurry. Be sure the command is understood.
- Consistency pays great dividends.
- Keep it simple; give single-word or two-word commands.
- Make each command clear, brief, and sharp.
- Never raise your voice and never lose your temper.
- If Bard refuses to perform a command, back up and give him another that he always performs, such as *come*. Then take a break and analyze the cause for his refusal.
- Don't try to reason with him.
- Teaching should be brief, in five- or ten-minute sessions once or twice daily.
- When a session isn't productive, forget it for a day.
- Never finish a session on a negative response.
- Never give a command that is impossible to perform.
- Don't forget Leadership Training discussed in the HOW-TO section at the end of this chapter.

---

frontation. Get his attention by speaking to him in gentle tones. Let him know that neither you nor he is being threatened or challenged. Tell him to sit because that will indicate to the approaching dog that Bard isn't taking a confrontational stance. Your companion will readily notice any negative posturing on your part and his guard will immediately be raised. Think

This Bullmastiff has mastered the sit-stay *command.*

training, with the possible exception of house-breaking. A treat might be a tiny cube of cheese or cooked meat, or a low-calorie commercial product. Bard responds to the flavor, not the size, of the treat that is offered to him, and he will learn his lessons with fewer problems if a small treat is offered routinely and quickly when each task is finished. Gradually substitute a verbal reward and a stroke of his head instead of physical treats, and by the time Bard is grown he will perform for your kind words of praise. Give him a tasty morsel at the end of the training session just to let him know you approve of his total performance.

Never Scold

Scolding is a form of punishment. When your Bullmastiff has done something bad, tell him *"Bard, no!"* in a normal volume, then wait a second for him to understand why the reprimand was voiced. Reserve the *no* command for times you want to eliminate an action, not when you are trying to modify a habit. Don't make a big deal about his mistake and don't attempt to explain his error. Never strike your pet, kick him, yell at him, or otherwise abuse him. Punishment is counterproductive when training any dog—with a giant breed it is also potentially dangerous.

Correction, Not Punishment

Correction is a positive action when it is applied in a loving way and without raising your voice. If Bard jumps up on a guest that has stepped into your living room, tell him *"Bard, sit."* If he doesn't respond to that command, call him to you, snap on his leash, and tell him *"Sit."* If necessary, enforce that command by placing your hand on his stern and pressing his bottom down while holding his collar with the other hand. That sequence needs no explanation, and you shouldn't issue verbal warnings to him or apologies to the guest. Make it apparent that you want Bard to behave and that you will take the necessary action to encourage appropriate behavior.

Teaching Simple Commands

To be effective, all commands should be kept simple. You should never give a command that you can't enforce manually except when using the "command as he does" technique. For example, anytime you see him running toward you, tell him *"Come."* If you see him sitting, tell him *"Sit,"* and if he starts to lie down, tell him *"Down."* This technique can be extended to

A bored Bullmastiff may chew to get attention.

housebreaking, but you will have to improvise your own commands.

Feeding Time Is the Right Time

The best time for a training exercise is immediately before Bard is fed. Soon he will accept training more readily because he knows that food will soon follow. When he first arrives at your home, turn him out into the backyard to investigate on his own for a while. Then step back into the house and put a small amount of food in his bowl. Step out the door with the bowl of food, call to him, *"Bard, come,"* and show the bowl in your hand; in all probability he will come running. Repeat that command every time he is fed and he will learn the three steps in the sequence:

1. His name is always called;
2. The recall command follows, *come*; and
3. He is fed.

Sit is an easy command to teach. Call him and after he has come to you, tell him, *"Bard, sit."* He won't know what you mean, so take a treat in your extended fingers, raise it an inch above his forehead, and place your other hand on his rump. Exert a tiny amount of pressure on his stern and slowly move the treat back over his eyes. As he follows the treat with his eyes, he will sit. Tell him, *"Good dog,"* and feed the treat. After sitting a minute, tell him *"Okay"* to release him from the command.

Down is another simple command he can learn at a very early age. Cause him to sit as described above, but instead of releasing him from sitting, take another tidbit and lower it until it is situated between his forepaws. He will probably lie down on his sternum, but if he doesn't, exert a slight pressure over his withers with your free hand, which should produce a down posture. Hold him there for a moment by showing him your flattened palm a few inches before his muzzle with your extended fingers touching each other. Wait a few seconds, treat him with a tidbit and a *"Good dog,"* then release him with an *"Okay."*

Healthy Exercise

Exercise and training are interrelated. When you toss a ball for Bard to fetch or you take him for a walk, you are exercising your companion as well as training him. You meet people and their dogs on your walk and socialization occurs naturally. Exercise is fundamental to the normal maturation of any dog, but it is a proven fact that a giant breed puppy must receive only moderate, low impact exercise. Bullmastiffs love walks but they do not make good joggers!

Short sessions of play should be interspersed with rest and relaxation.

Many positive factors are at work when a puppy plays, runs about, or walks on lead. Bard needs a certain amount of exercise to stimulate blood flow and nutrition to the soft tissues of the body, including his developing bone, cartilage, muscles, tendons, and ligaments. His physical strength and balance, as well as his mental agility and acuity, are also developing and require exercise. During exercise, lung capacity and function is enhanced and cardiac action is optimized. Short sessions of interactive play are healthy and necessary, and they intensify the bond between you and Bard. However, be especially careful to exercise him thoughtfully and cautiously until he has physically matured, at about eighteen to twenty-four months of age. *Don't let him become a couch potato, but don't press him to walk long distances.*

The Cost of Overexercising

Many of the aforementioned positive factors will be reversed by repeated, vigorous, and excessive exercise before maturity. Bard's young joints are at risk and injury can occur without your knowledge. Cartilage, soft bones, tendons, and ligaments are barely able to carry the rapidly increasing body mass of the giant puppy. Excessive exercise will demand more than those supportive structures can handle, sometimes resulting in irreparable deformities of the joints that can lead to permanent lameness or worse.

Until he is fully mature, do not encourage Bard to participate in vigorous activities such as racing, roughhousing, and playing with other dogs. If you wish to begin training for agility,

lower the bars to a few inches from the ground. If you ask him to jump obedience barriers, provide a soft footing and lower the barriers to a nominal height. If he initiates the exercise on his own, it is probably okay to let him romp, but his interactions with other dogs should be monitored and discouraged if he overdoes it. Playing with yard balls should be discouraged unless you are with him when he plays. Never leave another dog in the yard with your Bullmastiff puppy no matter what the occasion. Let him initiate his exercise and do not allow jumping and romping to get out of control.

Leadership training, formerly called dominance training, is critical when you invite a Bullmastiff companion into your home. It is never too soon to begin bonding, training, handling, leadershp training, and socialization. Instruction should begin the day Vicki arrives and some of it should continue into old age. Leadership training makes a significant impact in the bonding between owner and dog. It teaches Vicki her role in your home and identifies you as the dominant or alpha member of the pack. Leadership training lays the groundwork for teaching Vicki obedience to the family or pack leaders' commands. Abuse or heavy-handed training is neither necessary nor acceptable in the training program. No specific exercises are mandatory, but the following list provides a basis for establishing your leadership.

✔ Train Vicki gently, consistently, and always with enthusiasm. Speak in a moderate tone. (Shouting is no substitute for teaching.)

✔ Always provide a mat or soft rug for her to lie on, then insist that it be used.

✔ Brush her daily. She doesn't need that much grooming but it proves that you are the chief, the alpha leader of her pack.

✔ Never allow Vicki to sleep on your bed. That piece of furniture is reserved for the alpha leader.

✔ Feed her in a place other than the kitchen or dining room and after her human family has eaten. This will reduce temptation and teach her that the great-smelling food is for pack members that hold higher positions. It will also prevent her from snacking from your dinner when your back is turned, which may lead to more serious habits.

✔ If she begs for human food when snacks are served, confine her to another room or direct her to her pad and tell her "Down."

✔ Teach her to sit to receive treats, to be petted, or to be greeted.

✔ Move Vicki out of your way when she is sleeping on the floor.

✔ Occasionally when she's asleep on her special rug, move her off and sit on it yourself.

✔ Always take the lead when going through a door with her.

✔ Don't play tug-of-war with Vicki's toys because it tends to encourage aggressive behavior. Playing with a special tug-toy can be fun if you are strong and have good balance, but you should initiate the game and tell her when the game is finished.

✔ Don't respond immediately to Vicki's demands for play.

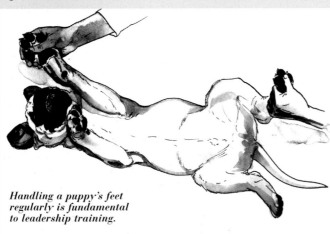

Handling a puppy's feet regularly is fundamental to leadership training.

TRAINING

Teach Vicki to sit quietly while her mouth is opened and her gums and teeth are examined. This leadership training will aid in brushing her teeth as well as teaching her place within the family.

Once in a while when she brings you a toy, don't accept it. Instead wait a few minutes; then get another toy and play.

✔ When you are finished playing with her toys, put at least one or two out of sight and out of her reach.

✔ Occasionally ignore Vicki for a few minutes when you return home. It will break your heart and she will be disappointed when you don't greet her immediately, but it will teach her to reserve her greeting until you are ready.

✔ Cause Vicki to lie on her back and rub her tummy. Lying on the back is a submissive posture.

✔ Stretch each leg, rubbing it from toes to thigh or shoulder.

✔ Gently pet and rub Vicki's tail.

✔ Rub her feet and separate her toes. Handle each one individually. This will help you train her for nail trimming.

✔ While sitting on the floor beside her, open Vicki's mouth and rub her gums. This will set the stage for later toothbrush use.

✔ Hold her mouth closed for a minute.

✔ Pick up each ear, look into the ear canals, and smell them. This establishes the attitude for future examinations and ear cleaning.

✔ Examine Vicki's eyes, but do not stare into them intently for more than a few seconds. You want to examine the character of the eyes but you don't want to antagonize her by staring.

✔ Stroke her entire body with a slicker brush.

All of these exercises should not be used every day and you should never continue any session longer than five minutes. After Vicki has fully matured and is found to be good natured and gentle, continue leadership training on a regular basis once or twice a week. If you see an attitude change beginning, increase the frequency and number of leadership activities.

GROOMING

Skin is the largest organ of the body. It reflects Vicki's general health, and much more. Having a short coat means that Vicki doesn't require as much combing and brushing as a double-coated Collie, but the same basic procedure is followed. Grooming is required for more reasons than coat appearance. When you groom your Bullmastiff, look carefully for abnormalities and meet them head on.

Reasons for Frequent Grooming

Vicki's puppy coat should be brushed daily with a grooming glove, nylon brush, or a rubber slicker. Daily grooming probably isn't necessary for coat health, but brushing your friend means personal hands-on care—the single most important function when bonding with your superb companion. Grooming is always accompanied by conversations and soon Vicki will expect your verbal communication. Brushing is a way to teach both dog and human roles in her new pack—another reason to give her a five-minute brush every day. Skin diseases aren't seen in Bullmastiffs any more often than any other breeds. However, if you brush her daily, you will

This beautiful Bullmastiff exhibits a well-groomed coat.

spot the signs of a problem much earlier than if you groom her less frequently.

Grooming Equipment

Buy a short-bristled brush, a grooming glove, or a rubber slicker. A grooming glove produces beautiful results and it adds a personal touch since you are actually petting her at the same time you inspect her skin for problems and slick down her glossy coat. A regular comb probably isn't necessary, but a flea comb serves a very useful purpose. You will appreciate the results of a final wipe with a soft, damp chamois cloth, which is available at any pet supermarket.

Nails

Vicki's nails will need trimming periodically, but no time schedule can be advised because

the nail growth rate varies in each individual. The frequency depends on her age, the surface where she walks, and how active she is. Her nails should be trimmed if they touch the floor when she is standing. Don't allow nails to grow too long or they will break off, and broken nails are never pleasant to care for.

Dogs' toenails are much like our own, except they are compressed laterally. A cross section of her nail-tip resembles an inverted *V*. Trim her toenail by nipping off the tip with a sharp scissor or guillotine-type nail trimmer. Then take another thin slice off the nail, then another.

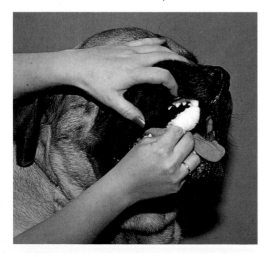

Nail trimming with a guillotine-type nipper.

When the nail becomes softer, your slices appear less hollow, and the *V* begins to close, you must stop. When the last cross section is taken, it will resemble an inverted *U* with its center nearly totally solid. That solid part of the nail contains tiny blood vessels and nerves. If you cut into it, the hemorrhage will be messy (but not dangerous) and the cut nerve will be quite painful to your companion.

Begin nail trimming as soon as Vicki is settled into the household routine. At first, trim her nails once a week to condition her to the procedure. After half a dozen trimmings, check her nails every few days and trim any that are too long. Buy a styptic stick at a pharmacy and if you cut a nail too short, press the dampened stick to the nail for a minute to stop the bleeding.

Ears

Vicki's ears are pendulant and therefore carry a slightly higher risk of infection than erect ears. Lift each ear and sniff for a musty, foul odor. Look in the outer canal for excessive wax or debris. About once a week, clean the outer canals with cotton dampened with hydrogen peroxide. If you detect a foul odor, or great accumulations of wax are found, make a veterinary appointment.

Teeth

Scrub her teeth with special dog toothpaste and a finger brush, available from a canine supermarket or a drugstore. Brushing is a habit that becomes more important later in Vicki's life, but brush her teeth three times a week

Teeth should be cleaned at least weekly.

when she is still a puppy to establish the procedure. As you open her mouth, look at her gums' character and color. They should be bright pink and moist. Her baby teeth will loosen, dislodge, and drop out at about three months of age, beginning with the front teeth (incisors), then the molars, and finally at about six months of age she will lose her long, pointed canine teeth. New teeth erupt as the deciduous teeth are lost.

Eyes

Because the Bullmastiff has loose facial skin, you should be alert to eyelid problems when you groom Vicki. Entropion, an inward rolling of upper or lower eyelids in one or both eyes, is occasionally a problem in the breed. It might be suspected when reddened eyes are squinting and watery. Entropion can be repaired by a veterinary surgeon; to ignore it may result in permanent corneal damage and partial or total blindness.

The wrinkled skin immediately below the eyes may collect dust and cause eye irritation. Clean the region around the eyes with a cotton ball moistened with water or saline solution available from a pharmacy.

Facial Folds

Infected flews: A Bullmastiff has flews, or multiple-fold, fleshy, pendulous upper lips. If these hanging folds are larger than normal, they may be intermittently wet from saliva and subject to infection that occurs in the deep recesses between the folds. Usually, this condition is called to your attention by a foul smell and the swelling and tenderness of the lip folds. Treatment usually includes gentle washing of the infected areas with cotton or a washcloth

A daily glance at your companion's face will alert you to loose skin problems.

TIP

Dry Skin

A dry coat that is dull and lacks luster may have several causes and should be promptly investigated.

✔ The problem may be related to infrequent brushing.

✔ Discuss the dog's diet with your veterinarian to be sure it includes ample fat and fat-soluble vitamins.

✔ Collect a fresh stool sample in a small zip-lock bag and take it to your veterinary clinic to check for intestinal parasites.

✔ If she hasn't been spayed, her estrous cycle may affect her coat quality.

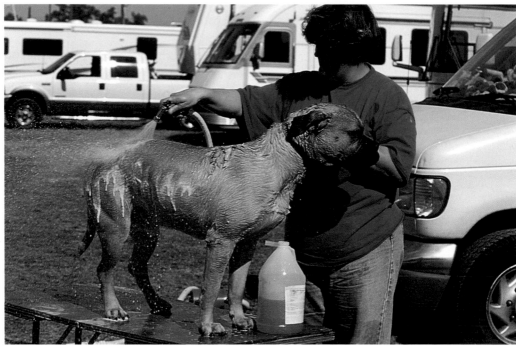

An outdoor bath is appreciated before a grueling day of Agility.

and bactericidal soap, followed by application of an antibacterial drying cream or powder. Preventive procedures should be discussed with your veterinarian if infection is recurrent.

Bathing Your Bullmastiff

Bathing Vicki is a two-person job that should be undertaken infrequently. A slick-coated Bullmastiff never needs bathing if she is thoroughly brushed several times a week. However if she finds a putrid animal carcass or something equally nasty, she may roll in it, and a bath may be necessary. You don't need any special equipment other than a handheld shower attachment on your bathtub faucet, and a slip-proof mat for her to stand on. Twist two cotton balls into long filaments and insert one into each ear canal. Put a speck of white petroleum jelly into each eye to protect her corneas from the soapy water. Fill the tub to her hock level with warm water and, with a friend's help, hoist her into the tub. Use the shower attachment to soak her coat but don't squirt water in her eyes or ears. Except for her face, lather her entire body with a good canine shampoo. Work the lather in for a few minutes and rinse her off with the shower attachment. Her face can be sponged off with a damp cloth after the bath. Dry Vicki with towels and if necessary, finish with a handheld hair dryer turned on the low-warm setting.

When brushed regularly, a Bullmastiff does not need frequent baths.

NUTRITION

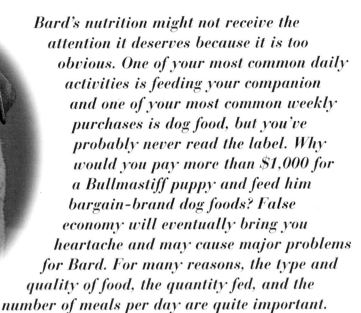

Bard's nutrition might not receive the attention it deserves because it is too obvious. One of your most common daily activities is feeding your companion and one of your most common weekly purchases is dog food, but you've probably never read the label. Why would you pay more than $1,000 for a Bullmastiff puppy and feed him bargain-brand dog foods? False economy will eventually bring you heartache and may cause major problems for Bard. For many reasons, the type and quality of food, the quantity fed, and the number of meals per day are quite important.

The Danger of Table Scraps

A common saying is "if it's good enough for me it's good enough for my dog." However, table scraps or leftovers from your meals are not balanced for canine nutrition. There are many reasons not to feed your dog human food, but a few will suffice.

• Milk will cause diarrhea in most canines, and cereal-milk with a trace of sugar commonly causes digestive upset.

• The sugar or salt content of human food, and the lack of or abundance of fiber, can cause digestive upsets.

Good nutrition is critical for fast-growing Bullmastiff puppies.

• Sweet, flavorful, or highly seasoned dressings or gravies are delicacies that humans love but they may cause serious problems in Bard's diet.

• Obesity is the bane of Bullmastiffs and can be caused by a table-scrap diet.

• Skin problems, digestive upsets, and vitamin and mineral deficiencies commonly are caused by feeding table scraps.

Better entrust Bard's diet to canine nutritionists with years of experience and technical knowledge. Those scientists formulate dozens of good diets that are continually tested to assure the finest ingredients. Remember, Bard is a valued companion, not an animated garbage disposal.

days, then 100 percent new food. While making the transition, be sure to note any food refusal, loose stools, or constipation.

Feed no fewer than three meals a day when he is a puppy: early morning, midday, and about an hour and a half before you retire for the night. Continue that schedule until he is about six months old, then switch to twice-daily feedings. Continue twice-daily meals until he reaches old age when you may want to switch back to three times per day. Do not leave the food out and allow Bard to eat when he chooses. That may initiate engorging, which in the Bullmastiff is terribly dangerous. Continue feeding two daily meals after he has reached adulthood—those meals will naturally be smaller than a single meal and smaller meals are important to prevent gastric torsion.

Overfeeding Dangers

How much should you feed your Bullmastiff puppy? Read the charts on dog food bags, but don't depend on them because they are only basic guidelines. In the beginning, follow Bard's breeder's advice. As the Bullmastiff gains weight, you must increase his meal size accordingly.

• If you have young children who occasionally feed Bard, ask them to record the amount and time they feed him. Yes, his treats are part of his daily diet and should be included.

• Keep a calendar near his food dish to record the quantity of each meal. Record each increase in quantity, his attitude toward his food, and any problems you notice. Record his weight once a week.

Dog Food and Feeding Frequency

When Bard first comes to your home, he should continue eating the same diet he was fed at the breeder's. Dietary changes may result in digestive upsets such as vomiting or diarrhea regardless of what food you substitute or how often he is fed. If you decide the breeder's diet isn't right for him after a week, mix 75 percent old food with 25 percent new for three days. Then mix 50 percent old with 50 percent new for a few days, then 25–75 for another few

Dog Food Label Definitions

AAFCO stands for the American Association of Feed Control Officials.

Amino acids are components of animal and plant proteins.

Animal feeding tests are AAFCO-controlled testing by canine feeding trials.

Bioavailability refers to the digestibility of a component.

Calcium is the percentage of calcium contained.

Calories are the amount of energy contained.

Carbohydrate is the total starch percentage including sugars and fiber.

Complete and balanced means that the food needs no vitamin or mineral supplementation.

Crude fat is the percentage of animal and plant fat.

Crude fiber is the percentage of indigestible carbohydrates contained.

Crude protein refers to the percentage of animal and plant protein contained.

Fatty acids are active components of fat.

Ingredients are listed beginning with the largest quantity and ending with the smallest.

Moisture content is the percentage of water contained.

NRC refers to the National Research Council, which publishes an excellent reference book called *Nutritional Requirements of Dogs.* It can be ordered by calling 1-800-624-6242.

Phosphorus is the percentage of phosphorus contained.

- His ribs should be easily palpated, and his skin should be supple and fit rather loosely. If his ribs are deep and soft, they are probably covered with fat and Bard's diet should be decreased or maintained without increasing for a few weeks.
- He should finish each meal within about five minutes.
- He should step back from his dish when it is empty. If he searches for more food, don't give him more immediately but consider increasing the size of his future meals.

This sleek, trim brindle Bullmastiff is neither overfed nor underfed.

A puppy should be weaned to a premium food specially formulated for its age.

• If he vomits food a short time after eating, it may be a sign his meals are too big. Continued or repeated vomiting is a sign of illness and should receive professional attention.

• Overfeeding will sometimes produce soft, slimy, or semisoft stools.

• His stool should be uniformly brown and any deviation should be investigated. Very light-colored or jet black stools are cause for concern. (Crayons seem to be attractive to big dogs and produce multicolored, kaleidoscopic stools that really get your attention. However crayons are not toxic and unless Bard is demonstrating abdominal distress, simply count

TIP

What to Look For

✔ Don't buy a food without considering the quality received for your dollar. Buy a *premium* dog food. It will cost more up front than the house-brand generics, but Bard will appreciate the taste and benefit from the nutritional value.

✔ Look for the AAFCO disclosure on the bag. Foods without the AAFCO declaration might be proven by feeding trials as well, but they require more research on your part.

✔ Food with a label stating that it meets the NRC maintenance recommendations shouldn't be used for growing puppies.

✔ Search the package for a toll-free number to call for answers to your questions about the food, its contents, and the type of feeding trials that are being used.

✔ Investigate the quality and source of the food's protein, fillers, coloring, and vitamin and mineral content.

✔ Make your choice and buy a small bag to check its palatability in Bard's dish. If he likes the taste and you like the formula and the price, invest in a large economy bag because it will be gone in a very short time.

the missing crayons and wait a day or two for his natural stool color to reappear.)

• If he is perpetually hungry but is maintaining his weight, reduce the quantity of each meal by a third, then add the quantity back in a fourth meal. That change might decrease soft stools as well.

A fawn Bullmastiff sniffs the air to discover what's for dinner.

Dog Food Types

Canned foods are costly when you consider they may contain as much as 70 percent water. Expense isn't the only problem. They can cause gastric distress because of the huge amount of water consumed in order to meet nutritional requirements.

Semi-moist foods are dehydrated and usually cause heavy water consumption. This can precipitate gastric problems and possibly torsion. Semi-moist foods sold in plastic pouches often appeal to humans because they look like meat. Be aware that the pouches also contain sugars and chemical preservatives that have caused allergic reactions. Thumbs down on pouch food!

Dry foods vary in quality from extra-bad to excellent. Dry food has become the standard for large breeds such as the Bullmastiff, and Bard will eat whatever food you buy if he is hungry.

Puppy Foods

Puppy foods are specifically formulated for growing pups. Canine nutritionists have determined the amount of protein, fat, and carbohydrate necessary for a puppy's normal growth and development, including many vitamins and minerals. A premium-quality puppy food should be a total diet for Bard throughout his growing years, eliminating the need for additional vitamin-mineral supplements.

Good nutrition is reflected by your companion's smooth and glossy coat.

Adult Foods

Maintenance diets contain adequate nutrition for adults who aren't under stress. The vitamin and mineral content will suffice for Bard under usual conditions when he isn't undergoing heavy training or work. You can start him on a maintenance diet safely after about eighteen months of age. Check with your veterinarian if in doubt.

Stress-Formula Diets

Seek a special diet during Bard's recovery from injury or illness, when he is pulling a cart or doing other work, or when he is training hard and under stress. Stress formulas include higher levels of bioavailable nutrients, which reduce the total quantity of food needed. These foods are usually formulated with increased vit-amins and minerals. They do cost more, but Bard is worth the expense. If your Bullmastiff is a female and is being bred, the stress formula can be used during pregnancy and lactation.

Supplements

Supplements should be added to premium food only if advised by your veterinarian. Protein, amino acids, fatty acids, and vitamins may be added to his premium diet if Bard has developed a particular need, such as a skin or coat problem. Supplements also may be recommended if he is recovering from a disease or injury. However, oversupplementation may interfere with nutritional balance and result in serious health consequences. Do not supplement Bard's diet with any product until you have checked with your veterinary advisor.

Treats

Most treats have calories and should therefore be considered part of Bard's diet. That is why commercial treat packages contain information similar to that found on dog food packages.

Give treats only for rewards and use them sparingly. Although you may want to treat Bard with occasional meat from the table, try to resist the temptation! Treat danger lies in the total quantity of treats Bard is fed, his reaction to those tasty tidbits, and your control over the situation. That danger is greatly reduced if Bard continues to eat his normal diet in a normal manner and maintains his weight. Ask the family to cooperate by recording the number of treats fed. Then reduce the quantity of treats given each day if the quantity is too great.

Bones contain calories too, but they are relatively few. A fresh, raw knucklebone from the butcher has many advantages for a growing puppy. Those bones rarely splinter and their ends are covered with cartilage that Bard likes to chew. Chewing strengthens teeth and jaws, aids shedding of deciduous teeth, and may continue for hours without significant nutritional effect. A bone is like a puppy tranquilizer that may keep your Bullmastiff occupied and out of mischief. The alternatives to fresh knucklebones are manufactured nylon bones and pressed rawhide bones. Don't give Bard twisted or knotted rawhide bones; after he chews them for a short time the remaining chunk can be swallowed and cause digestive problems. Read the labels carefully and consult with the breeder or your veterinarian if you have questions.

Bullmastiffs thrive on a balanced diet.

Cool water refreshes regardless of its source.

BULLMASTIFF ACTIVITIES

Vicki is a smart dog. She is well socialized with humans and other dogs and has excellent manners. She focuses on you every time you speak her name. Her horizons are limited only by your time and energy. However, that doesn't mean you must participate in every event your local Bullmastiff club has to offer. Vicki doesn't require extensive activities to make her happy and probably will be content to live in your house, follow you about, play a game of hide-and-seek, and perhaps take a walk down a shady lane once or twice a day.

How Do I Get Involved?

The following programs are just a few of the many structured canine pursuits available. All serve a useful purpose because they bring dogs and their people together for education or amusement. If you think Vicki and you might enjoy participating in some of the activities discussed, observe a training session before making up your mind. Rules and schedules of the activities can be obtained on the Internet

A well-adjusted Bullmastiff is a quiet dog that meets new challenges easily.

from the AKC Web page or that of the individual activity.

Canine Good Citizen Certificate

A Canine Good Citizen Certificate (CGCC) is a prized possession for a Bullmastiff and her owner. You will be very proud of Vicki as your trustworthy companion because she has been trained by you and judged by experts to pass the certification test. CGCC makes good sense for a giant like Vicki because it shows that a big pet need not be a big problem. The certifi-

Agility is a sport that Bullmastiffs thrive upon, but it does tend to be tiring.

cate framed on your wall signifies your determination and commitment to your dog's good manners and behavior and your insistence upon her correct comportment under all circumstances. CGCC testing isn't a formal AKC event, but it is sanctioned by the AKC and trained members of all-breed clubs do the testing. You don't compete with anyone; you simply teach Vicki how to act in ten different situations. You can train her without help, but classes usually are available and will benefit both you and Vicki—much of her success depends on human and canine interaction.

Review the general training suggestions in a previous chapter, obtain the specific testing

rules, and begin anytime you wish. Start the program at a young age, as soon as she behaves well on lead. You don't need to follow a strict time schedule—just move ahead with CGCC training at your own (and Vicki's) pace. Most parts of the test are situations that are easily worked into your socialization and training program.

One part of the test stresses your ability to control Vicki when you meet a friend on the street or in your home. In another exercise, you put Vicki in a sitting position at your side on lead, and an evaluator pets her on the head and body to test her manners. Another part of the test involves her appearance and grooming; the evaluator again approaches and inspects Vicki's coat, nails, and ears for cleanliness. She must sit quietly while he combs her lightly and picks up her feet one at a time. Another exercise tests your control and handling ability when changing directions while walking her. She is always on lead and is not required to walk at *heel*. Walking through a crowded street or mall is another skill that is tested, and sitting and staying *down* for a few minutes while on a long leash is another.

Other parts of the test include coming when called, reacting appropriately to another dog, and reacting to distractions such as shopping carts, wheelchairs, and bicycles. The final part is supervised separation wherein you hand the leash to the evaluator and leave Vicki's presence for three minutes.

Obedience trials are challenging, but a well-trained Bullmastiff takes the exercises in stride.

Obedience

Obedience trials are AKC regulated and usually held in conjunction with conformation shows. Obedience trials are judged in a structured manner and are formal continuations of Vicki's casual obedience training. An obedience trial demonstrates the usefulness of a purebred dog in the role of human companion. In order to score high, an obedience dog must not only be able to do what is asked of her, she must perform willingly and happily. She must execute the exercises quickly and correctly. She must focus on and be responsive to you, her handler, and demonstrate a high degree of interest in her endeavor.

The levels of an obedience trial are specifically designed with defined requirements to master before advancing to the next level. Trials are somewhat competitive, but certificates are awarded based on points earned regardless of the number of dogs in a trial. Obedience levels are Novice, Companion Dog (CD), Companion Dog Excellent (CDX), and Utility Dog (UD). Tracking is part of the UD level and can be continued as a separate endeavor. A dog without formal obedience training can participate in tracking dog events.

Obedience work requires a great deal of commitment from the handler, and to become efficient you must learn before you teach. You cannot train an obedience dog totally in your backyard even if you know the routine, rules, and technical definitions. Attend and join an obedience class taught by a local chapter of the ABA or your local all-breed club. These classes will teach you how to handle Vicki in an obedience trial and instruct you in the best ways to teach your companion to perform the obedience exercises correctly. Classes are made up of dozens of dog owners like you and many different breeds of both sexes. They give you and your Bullmastiff the opportunity to practice formal training in a community environment and goals to mark your progress in that worthwhile effort.

Agility

Agility may not be Vicki's cup of tea, but Bullmastiffs often participate in agility trials, a fun, timed activity that both you and she will enjoy. Sponsored by the AKC, agility trials are run off-lead and the competing dogs require intensive training. The competitor must find her way through an assortment of obstacles, run through tunnels, jump over barriers, walk elevated planks, climb up and over A-frames, weave through poles, and walk over a seesaw. You accompany her, waving her on and pointing to the next obstacle, but you can't touch her. The position of the obstacles varies from one place to another in different arenas.

Dogs must attain qualifying scores in one level before continuing to a higher level. Novice Agility (NA) is the first level, followed by Open Agility (OA), Agility Excellent (AX), and Master Agility Excellent (MX).

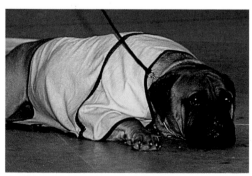

A therapy dog relaxes between visits.

Intelligence isn't the only requirement for an agility dog. No doubt Vicki can master the obstacles with minimal training and practice, but great speed is required to compete with super-athletic agility dogs, which are normally smaller than a Bullmastiff. Before you join a club and start training, attend an agility trial or two. If you decide to give it a try, obtain the rules and join an agility club to learn the ropes. You can build or buy the various props and train her in the backyard. Remember that the event itself is timed, so speed is the key.

Therapy Dog

Have you ever watched the face of an Alzheimer's patient light up when a dog appears in the care center? Have you seen hospitalized kids perk up when you hand them a ball to toss for Vicki to fetch? Some of the loneliest people on earth live in hospitals and senior citizen care homes, and the quiet demeanor of a Bullmastiff is made to order for visiting shut-ins. If Vicki is an outgoing dog, has a calm, sweet temperament, and has finished her CGCC training, you and she might enjoy brightening the lives of those who are less fortunate. A therapy or visitation dog must be docile and trustworthy, and if she likes to be petted and fussed over that will help. If you want your dog to brighten the lives of others, Vicki will do that by increasing the happiness of those she visits.

To prepare for therapy visitation, keep Vicki groomed, up to date on vaccinations, and certified by an organization such as the Delta Society, Therapy Dogs International, or local therapy groups. Some of these non-profit agencies provide liability insurance and tem-

Large dogs get fatigued more easily and need more time-outs than smaller dogs.

perament testing, and often they will evaluate the dog and handler. More extensive preparatory information is available on the Internet.

Conformation Showing

Dog shows might interest you and Vicki if she has a calm temperament and is an outstanding example of the breed. Conformation showing is an activity that appeals to professional dog breeders and those who are simply canine fanciers. In training classes offered to members of all-breed clubs and ABA members, AKC judges and professional handlers teach you the best way to exhibit Vicki. Even if you don't win the first time, you and Vicki will benefit from your training.

The ABA decides on the official standard for the breed. That standard lists all the important features possessed by a hypothetically *perfect*

Bullmastiff. The judge examines all the entries in the conformation class and selects the Bullmastiff that is the closest to the standard. Professional handlers travel the show circuits with their well-trained and beautiful dogs. Showmanship tricks abound in the rings and often influence the judges to a degree, but every now and then an unknown entry with superior conformation is discovered by a judge. If you have never attended an AKC conformation show, contact the ABA secretary to find the show nearest to you and go.

AKC Breed Standard

Reprinted with permission of the American Bullmastiff Association

General appearance—That of a symmetrical animal, showing great strength, endurance, and alertness; powerfully built but active. The

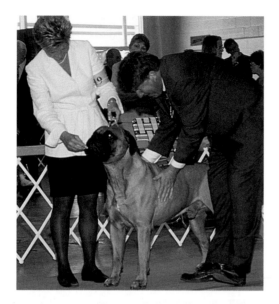

Beyond the typical dark mask lies a keen, alert expression.

Being judged in a show means being handled by a stranger.

foundation breeding was 60% Mastiff and 40% Bulldog. The breed was developed in England by gamekeepers for protection against poachers.

Size, Proportion, Substance—Size—Dogs, 25 to 27 inches at the withers, and 110 to 130 pounds weight. Bitches, 24 to 26 inches at the withers, and 100 to 120 pounds weight. Other things being equal, the more substantial dog within these limits is favored. Proportion—The length from the tip of breastbone to rear of thigh exceeds the height from withers to ground only slightly, resulting in a nearly square appearance.

Head—Expression—Keen, alert, and intelligent. Eyes—Dark and of medium size. Ears—V-shaped and carried close to the cheeks, set on wide and high, level with occiput and cheeks, giving a square appearance to the skull; darker in color than the body and medium in size. Skull—Large, with a fair amount of wrinkle when alert; broad, with cheeks well developed. Forehead flat. Stop—Moderate. Muzzle—Broad and deep; its length, in comparison with that of the entire head, approximately as 1 is to 3. Lack of foreface with nostrils set on top of muzzle is a reversion to the Bulldog and is very undesirable. A dark muzzle is preferable. Nose—Black, with nostrils large and broad. Flews—Not too pendulous. Bite—Preferably level or slightly undershot. Canine teeth large and set wide apart.

Neck, Topline, Body—Neck—Slightly arched, of moderate length, very muscular, and almost equal in circumference to the skull. Topline—Straight and level between withers and loin. Body—Compact. Chest wide and deep, with ribs well sprung and well set down between the forelegs. Back—Short, giving the impression of a well balanced dog. Loin—Wide, muscular, and slightly arched, with fair depth of flank. Tail—Set on high, strong at the root, and tapering to the hocks. It may be straight or curved, but never carried hound fashion.

Forequarters—Shoulders muscular but not loaded, and slightly sloping. Forelegs straight, well boned, and set well apart; elbows turned neither in nor out. Pasterns straight, feet of medium size, with round toes well arched. Pads thick and tough, nails black.

Hindquarters—Broad and muscular, with well developed second thigh denoting power, but not cumbersome. Moderate angulation at hocks. Cowhocks and splay feet are serious faults.

Coat—Short and dense, giving good weather protection.

Color—Red, fawn, or brindle. Except for a very small white spot on the chest, white marking is considered a fault.

Gait—Free, smooth, and powerful. When viewed from the side, reach and drive indicate maximum use of the dog's moderate angulation. Back remains level and firm. Coming and going, the dog moves in a straight line. Feet tend to converge under the body without crossing over, as speed increases. There is not twisting in or out at the joints.

Temperament—Fearless and confident yet docile. The dog combines the reliability, intelligence, and willingness to please required in a dependable family companion and protector.

Other Contests

Flyball is a timed event that is usually dominated by smaller, lightning-quick dogs. In flyball, the competitor runs full-tilt, jumps over bars, and steps on a pedal that opens a door

Young Bullmastiffs need plenty of attention and training.

from which a ball pops out. The competitor catches the ball, turns, and runs back to the starting line. Flyball is a truly spectator-pleasing sport but it doesn't really offer much to a quiet Bullmastiff.

Frisbee is another highly athletic contest in which the competitors jump to catch a Frisbee that the handler throws. Requiring quickness and innovative performance, it rarely attracts even the most playful Bullmastiffs. However, the contests are highly amusing to watch.

PROFESSIONAL HEALTH CARE

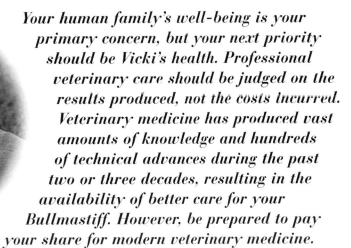

Your human family's well-being is your primary concern, but your next priority should be Vicki's health. Professional veterinary care should be judged on the results produced, not the costs incurred. Veterinary medicine has produced vast amounts of knowledge and hundreds of technical advances during the past two or three decades, resulting in the availability of better care for your Bullmastiff. However, be prepared to pay your share for modern veterinary medicine.

Home Examinations

While Vicki is still a puppy, perform a routine examination every day for a couple of weeks, then once a week for the next two months, and then once a month. Note your exam findings on the calendar where her vaccinations, heartworm treatments, and other parasite preventive measures are recorded.

• Pick up a fold of skin over her withers and release it. It should pop back to its normal position in a heartbeat. If it stands up like a teepee for more than a second, it means Vicki is dehydrated.

• Open her mouth and check the color and character of the mucous membranes of her gums, palate, and tongue. The membranes

The obvious curiosity of this young Bullmastiff indicates her state of good health.

should be pink and moist. Pale or dry gums denote problems.

• Check her teeth for food or other material lodged there.

• Check her nostrils for normal moisture. Dryness or discharge is abnormal.

• Her eyes should be bright, moist, and free of discharge. Squinting, angry red membranes, and green or yellow discharge are signs of problems.

• Look into her ear canals and smell them. Foul odor or excessive wax formation are signs of otitis and need professional follow-up.

• Pick up each foot and examine her nails for splits and excess growth. Her pads should be soft and pliable.

• Feel the joints of each limb and if swelling or tenderness is found, make appropriate notes and an appointment with your veterinarian.

Bullmastiff puppies need to be vaccinated.

• Check the color and character of Vicki's stool once every day. If it is white and chalky or loose and runny on two consecutive days, consult your veterinarian.

How Vaccines Work

A vaccine is administered to a healthy dog to prevent infectious diseases caused by *pathogens*. Viruses, protozoan elements, or bacteria may be disease-causing pathogens. A vaccine may contain dead or modified live pathogens, or a portion of a pathogen. The vaccine works by stimulating the dog's immune system to form *antibodies*. Antibodies seek and destroy a specific invading pathogen and protect the dog from a particular disease. Regardless of the virulence (potency) of the pathogen in its natural state, formation of a vaccine by modifying that pathogen also reduces the

The Vaccination Debate

• Canine vaccines are available for more diseases than ever before in history.
• Disease organisms (pathogens) are not universally distributed.
• All vaccines do not convey immunity in the same way.
• No vaccine is *perfect*.
• Some vaccines confer longer-lasting protection or a greater immune response than others, and some are more stable than others.
• A vaccine may cause undesirable reactions in some dogs.
• A vaccine may interfere with the positive effects of a different vaccine.
• Some dogs are unable to produce an immune response to some vaccines.

Before the use of immune testing, a common recommendation was to vaccinate for as many diseases as possible, beginning at the earliest age possible, and to boost all vaccinations annually. That "overkill" plan has protected millions of American canines for many years, but it may yield unpredictable results.

Some modern researchers hold that a better approach is to test for susceptibility to each disease before vaccinating against it. That plan, however, is fraught with technical and financial problems.

Unconditional victory for either side is probably not forthcoming in the near future. The American Veterinary Medical Association tells us that *disease risk* should be the primary factor to consider when choosing a puppy vaccination program.

reliability or duration of the immunity conferred by the vaccine. In other words, if a healthy dog contracts a specific disease and recovers from it without serious damage, that dog will probably be immune to that disease for life. Likewise, if a properly vaccinated dog is exposed to the live pathogen for which she was vaccinated, her immunity may be boosted. However, if she is vaccinated and not exposed to that pathogen for an extended period, her immunity will fade.

Passive Immunity

When antibodies are transferred from an immune donor to a healthy recipient, a passive immunity that lasts a few days or weeks will be conferred. An example of that phenomenon is when antibodies are passed from a bitch to her puppies. Some of her antibodies are donated to her unborn offspring via the placental attachment and more are passed in her colostrum (first milk). Those antibodies live for a limited time in the puppy and do not stimulate the production of more antibodies; thus, they confer no long-term immunity.

Active Immunity

When a vaccine against a pathogen is administered, the immune system immediately begins production of antibodies that will neutralize a subsequent invasion of that pathogen. This is called immune response and it results in active immunity. A newborn puppy's immune response is practically nonexistent because, even though the pup's immune system is in place, it isn't up and running until she is a bit

A puppy often harbors intestinal parasites. Only a stool test can tell for sure.

Core Vaccines

These core vaccines are needed by all dogs in most regions.
- Canine distemper virus (CD)
- Infectious canine hepatitis (CAV-1)
- Canine parvovirus (CPV)
- Canine rabies

Non-core Vaccines

Non-core vaccines are given to dogs with a higher risk of contracting the specific disease.
- Canine parainfluenza
- *Bordetella bronchiseptica*
- *Leptospira icterohemorrhagia*
- Lyme disease (*Borrellia burgdorferi*)
- Giardia
- Canine coronavirus

Healthy Bullmastiff puppies at play.

older, usually about eight weeks. By that time the passive immunity she received from her dam has diminished considerably. Thus, it is the best time to begin vaccination.

Combination Boosters

Some experts claim that boosters aren't needed except when test results indicate a low immunity to a particular disease. Others state that the cost of a combination booster vaccine is low compared to the cost of individual vaccines *and* tests, and that it is foolish to use anything except combination boosters. What is

best? Is the disease risk greater if you boost all vaccinations annually, or should a dog be tested for each disease annually and vaccinated only when the test dictates the necessity? What if a test result is skewed by a lab error? Can Vicki afford that risk? The best advice is to use common sense and personal knowledge about your dog. Work with a knowledgeable veterinarian and act according to his or her advice. Your veterinarian probably will discuss the core and non-core vaccines that are listed in the box on page 73. Be sure to advise your veterinarian about planned trips to other parts of the country.

Parasites

Many new drugs for parasite control are being developed. Only a limited discussion of their advantages and disadvantages is possible in the scope of this book.

Internal Parasites

Roundworms or ascarids are common intestinal parasites that are most harmful to puppies. The life cycle begins with the adult worm living in the intestine of a dog. A female ascarid lays thousands of eggs that pass out in the dog's stool. When another dog sniffs the stool, eggs are picked up, swallowed, and hatch into larvae that migrate in the host's body tissues. They eventually reach the lungs, are coughed up and re-swallowed, and mature in the intestine. Migrating larvae may remain in cysts in various parts of the body. If the host is a bitch that is bred, the larvae may continue their migration and infest the unborn puppies.

Hookworms are tiny blood-sucking worms that are also most harmful to puppies. Their life cycle differs somewhat from ascarids because the eggs hatch after leaving the host's body, and the larvae penetrate the puppy's tender skin. They migrate in the host's tissues until they reach the intestine where they begin their life cycle again.

Tapeworms are multi-host parasites that use many different animals, insects, and birds as secondary hosts. The adult tapeworm's head (scolex) attaches to the lining of the host's intestine. Tapeworms may reach several feet in length, and egg-like reproductive structures develop within segments of the worm. Segments break off and pass out with the stool, where they are eaten by a secondary host, perhaps a flea. The eggs develop in the flea's intestinal tract; when the dog eats the pesky flea, the eggs hatch and develop to adulthood, and the tapeworm life cycle begins again. Secondary hosts also may include deer and other wild animals.

Heartworms are horrible canine parasites that live within the host's heart and major blood vessels. Adult heartworms may reach many inches in length. In severe infestations the worms may compromise the heart's action, restrict blood flow, and threaten the host's life. Microscopic larvae (dirofilaria) are born to adult heartworms. These larvae are picked up by blood-sucking mosquitoes and are passed to other canine hosts when the mosquito feeds.

Apparently healthy adult dogs need regular veterinary checkups.

Preventable Infectious Diseases

Canine distemper (CD) is spread by contact with an infected dog or through airborne virus particles from coughs and sneezes. Symptoms are loss of appetite, thick yellow or green discharge from nose and eyes, lethargy, elevated temperature, muscle tremors, and convulsions. CD can cause paralysis and death. In very young puppies the only sign may be sudden death.

Canine hepatitis (CAV-1) may mimic distemper and cause sudden death. Its spread is similar to that of distemper. The disease eventually destroys the liver and causes death. Some affected puppies display cloudy corneas (blue eye) and impaired vision.

Canine parvovirus infection is easily spread by feces and other body discharges from infected dogs. It causes high fever, dehydration, heart complications, bloody and copious diarrhea, vomiting, and death. Recovery is sometimes possible with intensive therapy but aftereffects may linger. The virus may remain alive and infective for months in feces; it is difficult to kill and resists many common disinfectants.

Coronavirus appears similar to parvovirus and has many of the same signs and outcomes.

Lyme disease (borelliosis) is spread by blood-sucking insects such as ticks. It may cause systemic disease with fever, nonspecific pain, and lethargy. It also may cause severe or chronic joint pain, lameness, and lymph node swelling.

Kennel cough got its name from boarding kennels, where disease-ridden aerosol particles are spread like wildfire. It is caused by various organisms including bacteria like *Bordetella* and viruses like parainfluenza. It is an opportunistic coughing syndrome that lasts for weeks or even months, but is rarely life threatening unless the signs are ignored and a secondary infection arises.

Rabies is a fatal zoonotic disease (spread from animal to human). The virus lives in the salivary glands of infected animals and is spread by bites of those animals. Reservoirs of infection include coyotes, skunks, raccoons, bats, rats, ferrets, and mink. Occasionally rabies is also diagnosed in domestic cattle, dogs, and cats. Dog rabies vaccinations are required in most municipalities and confer excellent immunity. If a human is bitten by a rabid animal, immediate medical treatment is necessary.

Valley fever is a baffling zoonotic fungal infection of the arid Southwest. Spores produced by the fungus leave the infected dogs' bodies in their stools. Those microscopic spores can live in soil for eons and still be infective when another suitable host is encountered. Carried by the wind, spores may be ingested, inhaled, or otherwise contracted, and the resulting infection can cause chronic or acute signs. The fungal organism (*Coccidioides immitus*) reproduces in the host's tissues and may cause joint tenderness, lameness, respiratory distress, or a variety of other symptoms. The disease is sometimes hard to diagnose and very difficult to treat. Patients are often kept on medication for extended periods of time.

External Parasites

Mites are arachnids, eight-legged micro-scopic parasites that burrow in tunnels in the host's skin. A persistent reddened skin lesion, especially on Vicki's head, should alert you to the possibility of mite infestation. The pene-trated skin produces serum that oozes forth and supplies nutrition to the mite colony. Tunneling is also very irritating to the skin, and Vicki will scratch and rub the itchy skin patches, causing more irritation. If you find a raw, irritated lesion that is red and inflamed, especially in the facial region, call your veterinarian. Usually a skin scraping, viewed under a microscope, will reveal the species of mite that is causing the problem and your veterinarian will prescribe therapy.

Ticks also are arachnidan skin parasites, but they can be seen with the naked eye. They are abundant in spring and summer and their pre-ferred environment is grassy or wooded areas such as city parks and backyards. Male ticks are much smaller than females, but both sexes bury their heads in the host's skin and suck blood. An engorged female may swell to the size of a grape as she fills with blood. If ticks are not found, removed, and killed, the female will mate, drop off on the ground, and lay thousands of eggs. The eggs hatch into larvae, which molt to become nymphs, which molt into adult ticks. Two general varieties of ticks are found. One of the toughest to control is *Rhipcephalus san-guineus* (brown dog tick), a single-host parasite that infests and feeds upon dogs in all its stages. Most tick species are two- or three-host ticks that must find a different host species from which to feed at each stage of their life cycle.

Some ticks carry diseases (such as Lyme dis-ease) that can be transmitted to people, so be cautious when you remove a tick. Put on a

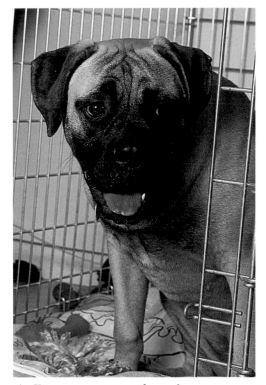

An X-pen serves as a refuge when rest is needed.

latex glove and grasp the tick with blunt tweezers close to Vicki's skin. Apply a slow, steady pull until the tick releases, then drop it into alcohol, which will quickly kill it. Mark the date on a calendar and consult your veterinar-ian if Vicki becomes ill a short time thereafter. Tick control should be discussed with your vet-erinarian and preventive measures taken by means of topical or oral drugs.

Fleas are very common, visible, wingless insects that are parasitic and contracted in infested environments. They are most plentiful in moist climates but they are occasionally

This is the safest way to transport your Bullmastiff(s) in a vehicle.

present in every region of the United States except at very high altitudes. A flea bites the skin and laps up serum as it exudes from the wound. The saliva of a flea is highly allergenic, which presents a major problem if Vicki develops an allergy to it.

Adult fleas inhabit Vicki's back. To help diagnose an infestation you may use a flea comb, which is just like any other steel comb except its teeth are quite close together. Begin combing just in front of her tail in a slow, steady pattern. Watch closely for fleas that are trapped between the comb's teeth. When one is found, you know that more than a hundred are pre-

sent on your Bullmastiff and that 10,000 immature forms are living in her environment.

If you do not have a flea comb, use your fingers to repeatedly part Vicki's hair on her rump or under her collar and search for tiny black specks of flea feces. If found, place the crumbly black speck on a white paper towel and moisten it with a drop of water. Flea feces will turn red because of its blood content. If those diagnostic methods yield no positive results, turn Vicki over and search for the scampering parasites on her belly and groin areas.

Female fleas mate and lay eggs that drop off and molt on the carpet, grass, or any other convenient place in the environment. Flea larvae eat about any organic matter available and after molting several times, the adults can live without a blood meal for months.

Bathing Vicki using an insecticide flea shampoo will provide immediate relief, but bathing is not a good method of long-term control. Discuss the infestation with your veterinarian and decide which of the many new flea control methods are best suited to Vicki and you. It is possible to control flea infestations by interrupting the life cycle of the pest, but the specific product used will depend on whether the infestation is seasonal or year-round.

Lice are skin parasites as well, but they have more stable life cycles and are easily treated. Lice are transmitted from dog to dog by contact. Unlike fleas and ticks, lice live totally on the infested animal. Tiny white eggs (nits) are attached to Vicki's hairs, usually along her back. Adult lice suck blood from the host, causing intense itching. Parasiticide baths at weekly intervals will aid in controlling lice.

Ear mites are nearly microscopic in size but they can be seen with a hand magnifier. They look like tiny white dots scurrying around on a piece of black earwax that has been extracted from Vicki's ear canal. Ear mite infestation causes intense itching, head shaking, scratching at the ears, and even whining and crying. Usually that means a trip to your veterinarian for diagnosis and ear cleaning followed by home therapy. Ear mites are contagious to other pets and they frequently cause repeated problems.

Skin fungus. The most common one is *Microsporum canis*. It is sometimes called ringworm, although it may not form a ring and it is not a worm. Fungus infection should be suspected in cases of reddened, hairless patches accompanied by intense itching, especially on Vicki's belly. Fungi are plant organisms that multiply and spread by producing spores that act like seeds. Suspected fungus infestations should be referred to your veterinarian, who may diagnose the condition by sampling the lesion, culturing it, and examining it under a microscope. Therapy may be topical or systemic, and it may take several months to abate a serious infestation.

Noncontagious Skin Conditions

Hot spots are localized bacterial skin infections that are seen most frequently in long-haired dogs. The infection often follows one of the discussed parasite infestations. Usually a hot spot is treated both topically and systemically and relief is quickly attained.

Calluses may lead to decubital ulcers or bedsores, which may become infected when Vicki is an old lady if she isn't given soft pads to lie on.

The wrinkled face of a Bullmastiff predisposes it to numerous skin problems.

Elbow hygromas are pockets of serum that collect beneath Vicki's skin as a result of dropping to her elbows on hard floors. Hygromas sometimes become infected and require professional attention, but if you discover them early, they can be averted by investing in a few soft pads and placing them in her favorite napping places.

Hereditary Diseases

Arthritis is a joint inflammation and is quite common to Bullmastiff seniors, even if their hips and elbows are certified normal. The high incidence may be caused by stress on joints related to the weight of the individual. Obesity and lack of regular, modest exercise will increase that stress.

Dental tartar can cause gum erosion, tooth loosening and loss of teeth, and gingivitis (gum infection). Dental neglect may lead to kidney failure or heart disease. It is easily prevented by appropriate dental care throughout life. Brush Vicki's teeth twice a week when she's a puppy. Later in life, if you see a bit of tartar building

Like other very large breeds, the Bullmastiff is subject to deadly gastric dilation and volvulus.

up in spite of your efforts, take her to your veterinarian for examination and dental scaling. Chewing nylon or pressed rawhide bones will help prevent tartar.

Allergies are seen in many Bullmastiffs and must be evaluated on an individual basis.

Tumors are common to Bullmastiffs and are classed as benign or malignant. Benign tumors include skin cysts, gum tumors, and fatty tumors. One of the most serious malignant tumors is osteosarcoma, or bone cancer. If you find rapidly changing lumps, bumps, or erosions on Vicki's body, make an appointment with your veterinarian to check them.

Gastric dilation, torsion, and volvulus (GDV) is on the rise in the United States. It is always an emergency—immediate veterinary treatment is needed because the condition may progress rapidly to an irreversible, fatal conclusion.

Signs of that horrible event include bloating, especially on the left side behind the rib cage, usually accompanied by difficult breathing, darkened mucous membranes, copious salivation, unproductive vomiting attempts, disorientation, and coma. Death may occur within an hour from the onset of signs.

Vicki's physical size and natural eating and drinking habits predispose her to GDV. Large, infrequent meals also can precipitate GDV as well as vigorous exercise and engorging on water immediately after eating. Preventive measures include feeding several small meals per day. Vicki should not be allowed to drink great amounts of water immediately after eating, and her activities and excitement should

Many genetic diseases can't be diagnosed until your companion reaches maturity.

be curtailed for an hour after each meal. There is a current debate about the value of elevating her food bowl to chest height. A Purdue University study indicates that a happy, well-adjusted temperament may decrease the incidence of GDV.

Hereditary eye diseases include progressive retinal atrophy (PRA), glaucoma, retinal dysplasia, and entropion. PRA and retinal dysplasia are deterioration diseases of the retina. Glaucoma is increased pressure within the eye that also destroys the retina in time. Entropion is the inward rolling of the upper eyelid, lower eyelid, or both. That condition can be cured by a relatively simple surgical procedure.

Canine hip dysplasia (CHD) is a hereditary disease that occurs in many purebred dogs. It refers to abnormal formation of the ball-and-socket hip joint, which predisposes dogs to joint remodeling, arthritis, pain, and lameness.

Various surgical procedures are used to relieve pain or deformity; in milder cases, anti-inflammatory drugs are somewhat effective. Sometimes therapy is futile because of joint stress, arthritis, and degeneration caused by the weight of the Bullmastiff. Total hip joint replacement is possible but very expensive and not always effective.

Elbow dysplasia is a hereditary disease involving the lower end of the humerus and the upper ends of the radius and ulna. Various degenerative changes occur, and the degree of pain and lameness depends upon those changes. Sometimes surgical procedures will relieve the condition, and in milder cases, anti-inflammatory drugs will relieve pain.

Other genetic problems that are reported include heart diseases, hypothyroidism, miscellaneous skin diseases, shortened tails, screw-tails, and cleft palates. Also reported is cervical

Hot weather means a Bullmastiff seeks shade and comfort.

vertebral malformation, which can cause various serious syndromes that are related to the upper spinal development of puppies from three to five months of age. Ataxia, or the inability to walk, is occasionally seen in very young puppies between four and ten weeks of age and is believed to be a type of cerebellar (brain) degeneration.

Control of Hereditary Diseases

Hereditary diseases are only controllable by conscientious breeders who keep their eyes and minds open. Most reputable Bullmastiff breeders are trying to improve the breed with each litter they produce. When they are successful, those deformities and diseases gradually diminish. Pet owners should buy puppies from breeders who test their breeding stock and choose the very best parents possible. Never buy from a vendor who can't produce documentation of brood-stock testing.

Emergencies

Bullmastiffs usually are housedogs. They don't dash about in heavy brush to flush out a few quail, nor do they plunge blindly into lakes and streams to pick up wounded ducks. Vicki probably never will be wounded and hopefully she never will have need of emergency treatment. Excellent training and control of your companion will prevent car accidents and fight wounds, but you should be prepared for a few emergencies.

Heat Stroke

A serious problem may occur if you leave Vicki inside a car for more than a few minutes. Heat stroke can occur in the winter if the sun shines through the windshield and windows, and it may occur in the summer even if some windows are left open. Don't assume that Vicki's short coat will prevent her body temperature from skyrocketing when subjected to the oven-like heat of a car. In a very few minutes her body temperature may rise from 105–110°F (41–43°C). Signs of heat stroke include open-mouth breathing, bright red oral membranes that soon become pallid, thick, stringy saliva, coma, and death.

First aid for heat stroke includes cooling Vicki with a garden hose or a tub of water. Don't use ice or ice water because that will cause vascular constriction and may worsen the condition. Encourage her to drink but don't pour water into her mouth if she is comatose. Prevention is more productive than the best therapy. To avoid heat stroke, follow these tips:
✔ In a hot climate, put a children's play pool filled with water in Vicki's backyard.
✔ Be sure she has fresh water available at all times.

This young Bullmastiff's leg bones may be fractured if she falls from a porch or someone's arms.

✔ Allow her the freedom to seek shade and cool grass. Never tie her up.
✔ Never leave her in an automobile when you aren't with her.

Wounds

In the unlikely event that Vicki receives a serious wound by stepping on broken glass, use a T-shirt or sock to wrap her foot tightly enough to curtail the bleeding. Call your veterinarian to say you are on your way. If unable to stop the bleeding with a pressure bandage, place your belt, necktie, or shoestring around the leg above the wound and tighten it just enough to stem the hemorrhage.

Fractures

Housedogs don't often suffer fractured bones, but in case Vicki is accident prone and falls from the top porch step, here's what you do. Don't pick her up; instead examine her where she lies. If her leg is abnormally bent, don't attempt to straighten it. Send someone for a makeshift stretcher such as an ironing board, door, or other large, flat object. You and your helper should carry her on the stretcher to your car, slide her onto the back seat, and proceed to the veterinarian's office. Leave her on the seat and let the veterinary technicians take it from there.

To Breed or Not to Breed

Why should you breed your Bullmastiff? Only one answer satisfies that question. If your Bullmastiff has a flawless disposition, passes all hereditary disease testing, and meets all color, temperament, and conformational criteria with few deviations from the breed standard, he or she might be considered as a contributor to the breed's gene pool.

If you bought a Bullmastiff as a family pet, a companion for you to spend some quality time with, to enjoy and appreciate daily, you've already answered the question of whether or not to breed. Those are strong arguments against breeding, which involves ring-training and comparing your companion to the finest Bullmastiffs around. That means spending many hours of your time and money preparing your dog and yourself for dog shows. It means professionally judged conformation and disposition showing against that of his peers. It means wins in show competition with the best Bullmastiffs in the region, where only the top contender is chosen to wear the purple ribbon.

A prospective breeding Bullmastiff should have a great personality and terrific train-

Owning a pair of Bullmastiffs doesn't mean you must raise puppies.

ability. The dog must be trustworthy, quiet and calm, friendly and protective.

If you decide to stand Bard at stud, keep in mind a few warnings:

1. Better have deep pockets before you start. To prove his quality in the conformation ring, you must be able to cover the cost of shows, handler's fees, and transportation to and from shows.

2. The cost of providing health and dietary care for a brood bitch and her litter is likewise significant. Consider her food, the puppies' food, the prenatal and post-whelping exams, possible X-ray or ultrasound imaging, the whelping box, and vaccinations for dam and puppies. Don't forget your time spent cleaning up after a litter for a couple of months and searching for appropriate puppy homes.

3. Bullmastiff bitches have a relatively high dystocia rate (whelping problems), and many must receive professional help. Many litters are delivered by cesarean section, which is a costly procedure.

4. The risk of cesarean section is minimal if the dam's health and condition are superior but surgery always presents a calculated danger. That risk must be added to the uncertainty of owning an intact bitch. Pyometra, mammary cancer, and other serious diseases are common to unspayed bitches.

5. Owners sometimes breed a Bullmastiff to recoup their original cost. Forget that! Reputable Bullmastiff breeders don't make a lot of money by breeding. They strive to improve the breed by producing sound and steady puppies and, once in a while, to stand alongside a winner in the

A Bullmastiff will live a longer, happier life if it is spayed or castrated as a puppy.

trophy ring. Their avowed purpose is to breed a fine bitch to a fine stud and, perhaps, to produce a pup that is better than either parent.

Spaying a Female

Known as spaying, ovariohysterectomy means surgical removal of the uterus and ovaries. Reasons to spay a female before her first heat are too numerous to count, but here are a few:

1. Spaying prevents three-week-long estrous (heat) cycles twice a year and prevents the possibility of inadvertent breeding.

2. A bitch in heat is a nuisance because she attracts the male dogs of the neighborhood to your door and leaves bloody evidence of her condition each time she sits on the carpet.

3. Spaying before the first heat virtually prevents mammary cancer.

4. Spaying may calm an otherwise aggressive personality.

5. Spaying precludes pyometra, a dangerous form of uterine infection, which may threaten the bitch's life.

6. Spaying does not affect the bitch's temperament, personality, or trainability.

Neutering a Male

Castration, or neutering a male, means surgical removal of both testicles. Reasons for castrating a young male are nearly as important as those for spaying a female.

1. A castrated male is usually less aggressive toward other dogs and people.

2. Prostate cancer and testicular tumors do not occur in a castrated male.

3. A castrated male is happy and content in a family environment and rarely tries to escape to find a female in heat.

4. Neutering a male at any age does not cause adverse changes in temperament, personality, or trainability.

Spaying a female or neutering a male doesn't cause obesity. Dogs get fat for the same reasons that people do; they consume more calories than their bodies burn. Overfeeding causes most cases of obesity, but medical conditions also can cause dogs to store their calories. If your Bullmastiff becomes overweight, take him to your veterinarian for diagnosis; if he is healthy, begin a logical course of nutritional management.

Veterinary practitioners are not clones. They come from all walks of life, they have been educated in different colleges and universities under varying influences, and their practice experiences vary. Basic book-knowledge is much the same for all graduate veterinarians but application of that knowledge and advanced education are quite individual.

When you are deciding which doctor of veterinary medicine to entrust with Vicki's health, the first factor to consider is that you *do* have a choice—if a relationship is not fruitful, you are free to change doctors.

Call a few animal hospitals in your area. You can learn a good deal about a practice and the quality of service provided from the interest displaced by the telephone receptionist. If the person on the phone takes your name and offers to have a professional speak with you to answer your questions about the practice, that's good.

Explain to the operator, technician, or veterinarian that you have acquired a Bullmastiff puppy and wish to have Vicki examined by a professional, but first you want to visit the hospital and meet the staff. Take a pad and pencil and write down your findings on your tour.

• Note the number of technicians and helpers. Are they clean, friendly, and presentable? Are they so numerous that they overwhelm you, or does each have a particular job that is done efficiently?
• Does the hospital smell clean? A certain amount of animal odor must be excused because a busy practice sees dozens of pets, and hospitalizes some of them, each day. Cats must use their litter trays, sick and injured dogs aren't always clean, and exercise runs can't always be washed after every use.
• Equipment cleanliness and maintenance should have a high priority.

Always keep tight control of your dog at the veterinarian's office, where she is exposed to other dogs and pets.

• Uniform and smock cleanliness reflects personal and professional pride.

Before leaving, try to speak with the veterinarian who handles most of the giant dogs and size up the clinician with whom you consult. Is the veterinarian anxious to meet Vicki and willing to discuss your questions frankly and without reservation? Be sure to ask about

✔ the number of Bullmastiffs and other giant breeds seen

✔ OFA X-ray certification, both elbows and hips

✔ the routine for CERF examination and certification

✔ after hours calls and who takes them for the practice

✔ gastric torsion and volvulus prevention and treatment

✔ facilities for overnight hospitalization

✔ nutritional and dietary supplement concerns

✔ the amount and nature of exercise for your Bullmastiff

✔ a vaccination schedule and the veterinarian's view of vaccine types and usage

✔ internal parasite detection and treatment options

✔ reasons for and against spaying or castration, and the best age for the procedure

✔ fee schedule, including vaccinations, routine surgery, hospitalization, office visits, after-hours calls, and house calls

✔ trainers in the area who have the most experience with giant breeds

If you aren't impressed with either the professional consultation or your findings in the hospital, don't make an appointment for Vicki's examination. Visit another facility and repeat

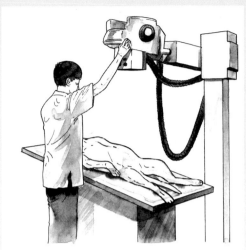

Your Bullmastiff may be X-rayed for hip dysplasia at two years of age.

your investigation. Find a likeable veterinarian who practices in an above-average, clean environment, and who converses openly with you.

You should be able to find an honest, positive personality with a soft, easygoing tableside manner—a clinician who exudes professionalism, not a disinterested veterinarian who is reluctant to touch and handle your Bullmastiff. Pick a veterinarian by similar criteria as you would when choosing a friend for yourself. Seek a practitioner with a quiet sense of humor, firm handshake, thoughtful answers to your questions, and a pleasing, frank, and informative manner.

Find a veterinarian who has excellent knowledge but isn't afraid to consult textbooks or the opinion of other experts. Beware of veterinarians who frown at every suggestion you offer and those who scoff at new ideas or alternate procedures.

YOUR AGED BULLMASTIFF

Aging problems are inevitable, and big dogs age more rapidly than tiny breeds. Old dogs, like old people, have a few special needs that an owner should provide. Your goal should be to make your Bullmastiff's declining years as comfortable and enjoyable as possible.

Routine Physical Examinations

The average life span of a Bullmastiff is estimated to be eight to ten years but many succumb to cancer before they have time to realize the joys of senior living. After reaching seven years of age, Bard should have a professional examination twice a year. Those exams will pay for themselves if the veterinarian discovers even one problem that wouldn't have been noticed otherwise.

Your veterinarian will look into Bard's mouth for dental problems, check his ears for infections, examine his eyes, and go over his skin for cysts and tumors. The clinician will palpate his joints for swelling, search for signs of malig-

Your companion may contract various old-age problems that can be alleviated if caught in time.

nancies, and watch his gait. Usually, an inexpensive physical exam is all that is needed, but lab work may be done if a problem is suspected. Don't leave the veterinary office without an explanation of lab work ordered and the significance of each new finding.

Dietary Adjustments

Don't change dog foods just because your pal has reached golden oldie status. If advised to change, be sure you understand why the change is indicated. A particular diet may be needed to address a specific problem or to improve Bard's general condition. A cardiac diet may be recommended to address signs of congestive heart failure, or a kidney diet to compensate for kidney impairment. A low-calorie diet might be used to address obesity, or a geriatric diet to supply more vitamins, higher-quality protein, and more digestible food.

Weight loss may occur; if it progresses rapidly, laboratory tests might be indicated to diagnose the cause. If the test results are normal and Bard is being fed twice daily, try feeding him three, smaller meals per day. If he is disinterested in his food, try soaking it in half a cup of warm beef or chicken broth.

Water Consumption

Old dogs often develop a greater need for water, but that is not necessarily a disease symptom. Put a bowl of fresh, cool drinking water near each of Bard's favorite napping places. Excessive water consumption might be a sign of kidney compromise, diabetes, or other disease. If the quantity consumed is excessive, measure the amount he drinks from each bowl and report to your veterinarian. A urinalysis and blood profile will rule out various diseases and a special diet or specific therapy can be started.

Urinary Incontinence

Loss of urinary control is the bane of many old female Bullmastiffs and some males as well. After Bard has been examined and laboratory results have ruled out disease conditions, his problem may be simply a loss of muscular control of the bladder. Incontinence isn't the end of the line for your old Bullmastiff. You can deal with that inconvenience by taking him out more frequently and changing his food according to your veterinarian's advice. Visit thrift shops and buy several bath mats. Those thick, rubber-backed mats will serve several purposes for your elderly Bullmastiff. They provide fine resting places for the old guy and can be tossed into the washer when damp.

Senile Dementia

Dogs are not known to suffer from Alzheimer's disease, but senior canines may present mental problems and forgetfulness, called cognitive dysfunction. Bard may wander aimlessly, as if seeking something in particular. He may choose new resting places, a new toilet area, or he won't remember where his water bowl is located. Have patience with your old pet. Don't scold or punish him for forgetting.

Failing Sight and Hearing

Nuclear sclerosis that resembles cataracts is common in older Bullmastiffs. Many afflicted dogs continue to manage extremely well in spite of their diminished vision. If Bard's vision isn't as sharp as it was, toss his ball slower or bounce it in front of him. Take him over curbs cautiously so he doesn't stumble. Don't ask him to walk through underbrush or on difficult trails. Build a ramp up the back steps so he doesn't need to navigate the stair risers. Above all, don't move the furniture around inside your home.

Senile deafness is also a simple problem to handle. Don't sneak up on Bard. Make your approach known by stomping your feet so he will feel the vibration. Pet and touch him frequently when taking him for a walk. His sense of smell probably won't fail, and as soon as he scents your presence he will be reassured.

Comfort Aids

Thrift store bath mats will pad Bard's old, arthritic joints and may even prevent decubital ulcers or hygromas. If you know he is having difficulty rising, he will appreciate help getting to his feet. Slide your hands under his rump and slowly lift him to a standing position.

Letting Go

The *only* loving and kind motive for euthanasia is Bard's inability to enjoy life any longer. Signs of old-age debility are many; when one more is added to your dog's long list, you may want to discuss euthanasia with your veterinarian. When that time comes, face it with courage and determination. Think of Bard's lifelong devotion to you and your family and remember the courage he demonstrated thousands of times. Then ask yourself and your veterinary advisor if you should wait until one more problem arises.

Euthanasia: How, When, and Where

Euthanasia is painless and positive if done correctly by professionals. To avoid the confusion of waiting in a room with other pets, ask your veterinarian to come to your home or to meet you at the veterinary hospital before or after office hours. Give your old companion lots of loving reassurances when the time arrives. If you aren't excessively emotional, stay with him through the event. If you can't handle the grief, ask another member of your family to be there instead. The veterinarian will quickly slide the needle into Bard's vein, rapidly inject the lethal solution and your old companion will quietly drift off to sleep and never awake.

Picking Up the Pieces

Saying goodbye to an old friend for the last time is never pleasant. Ask your veterinarian or local dog club for the name of a support group

Senior Bullmastiffs need special consideration in their old age.

to help you through your grief. Don't even attempt to forget Bard's personality, his strength, and his youthful vitality. If you are a camera buff, put his snapshots in an album. Take the family to a nursery and select a small, sturdy tree to plant in his honor in your yard or in a nearby park. That arboreal headstone will be a living reminder of Bard's life and the love and companionship you shared with him.

Books

Alderton, David. *Dogs.* New York, NY: DK Publishing, Inc., 1993.

American Kennel Club. *The Complete Dog Book, 18th Edition.* New York, NY: Simon & Schuster Macmillan Company, 1992.

Beaver, Bonnie V. *Canine Behavior.* Philadelphia, PA: W.B. Saunders Company, 1999.

Coile, Caroline D. *Encyclopedia of Dog Breeds,* Hauppauge, NY: Barron's Educational Series, Inc., 1998.

Rice, Dan. *Big Dog Breeds.* Hauppauge, NY: Barron's Educational Series, Inc., 2001.

Von der Leyen, Katharina. *140 Dog Breeds.* Hauppauge, NY: Barron's Educational Series, Inc., 2000.

Yamazaki, Tetsu and Kojima, Toyoharu. *Legacy of the Dog,* San Francisco, CA: Chronicle Books, 1995.

Bullmastiff Web Sites

The American Bullmastiff Association
www.bullmastiff.us

ABA Bullmastiff Rescue Service
www.bullmastiff.org/rescue.htm

American Kennel Club
Bullmastiff Breed Standard
www.akc.org/breeds/bullmastiff/index.cfm

Important Note

Most Bullmastiffs are quite docile and rarely cause damage to people or property unless the dogs are teased, abused, neglected, or allowed to run loose. However, to be sure that your homeowner's policy adequately covers your needs, tell your insurance agent that you own a Bullmastiff, and follow the insurance company's advice about coverage. About 500,000 to 1 million dog-biting incidents occur annually in the United States. Liability claims involving dog attacks reach $250 million to $1 billion per year. Dog bites now are the second reason for emergency room admissions according to the Centers for Disease Control (CDC), and most of the approximately 20 annual dog-bite fatalities involve children less than 10 years old. That information is intended to wake you up to reality! You need to train and control your dog from the very first day!

This guy's expression indicates a desire for more creature comforts.

Assorted expressions of contented, curious Bullmastiffs waiting for playtime.

About the Author

Dan Rice obtained a unique understanding of companion pets and their owners through a long personal and professional association with clients and patients. Writing was a hobby most of his professional life and after retiring from active veterinary practice he embarked on a serious writing career. Endless reading and researching purebred dog breeds and their idiosyncrasies maintain his knowledge of the dog fancy. *Bullmastiffs* is his fifteenth book published by Barron's. Other titles include *Bengal Cats, Complete Book of Dog Breeding, Complete Book of Cat Breeding, Akitas, Dogs from A to Z, The Well-mannered Cat, Brittanys, Training Your German Shepherd, The Dog Handbook, The Beagle Handbook, Big Dog Breeds, West Highland White Terriers,* and *Small Dog Breeds.*

Acknowledgments

My sincere gratitude goes out to Editor Pat Hunter, Acquisitions Editor Wayne Barr, and all the staff at Barron's Educational Series for giving me the privilege of writing *Bullmastiffs.* I salute ABA Secretary Lindy Whyte, Bullmastiff expert and breeder, and Bullmastiff breeder and trainer Jenny Baum with a hearty thank you for proofreading part of the manuscript and offering their expert advice. Thanks also to breeders Betty Ruffini and Kathy Gladden who contributed their opinions and information. As always, I'm indebted to my soul mate Marilyn for her expert help and patience while working on this project

Photo Credits

Norvia Behling: pages 36, 44, 60, 62, 71, 72, 73, 83, 85, 91, 93 (bottom right); Kent Dannen: pages 18, 19, 23, 25, 29, 38, 39, 40, 43, 57, 61 (both), 63, 64, 66, 68 (top), 78, 80, 93 (top); Tara Darling: pages 7, 14, 20, 24, 28, 30, 45, 50 (both), 58, 59, 74, 79, 82, 88; Isabelle Francais: pages 5, 6, 8, 10, 13, 17, 26, 27, 31, 34, 35, 37, 49, 52, 53, 54, 56, 65, 67, 68 (bottom), 70, 75, 77, 81, 89, 93; Pets by Paulette: pages 3, 4, 11, 32, 48, 51, 55, 69, 84, 92

Cover Photos

Front cover: Isabelle Francais; back cover and inside front cover: Pets by Paulette; inside back cover: Kent Dannen

All inquiries should be addressed to:
Barron's Educational Series, Inc.
250 Wireless Boulevard
Hauppauge, NY 11788
www.barronseduc.com

ISBN-13: 978-0-7641-3304-6
ISBN-10: 0-7641-3304-7

Library of Congress Catalog Card No. 2005045388

Library of Congress Cataloging-in-Publication Data
Rice, Dan, 1933–
    Bullmastiffs : everything about purchase, care, nutrition, health care, and behavior / Dan Rice.
        p. cm. — (A complete pet owner's manual)
    Includes bibliographical references and index.
    ISBN 0-7641-3304-7
    1. Bullmastiff. I. Title. II. Series.

SF429.B86R53   2006
636.73—dc22   2005045388

Printed in China
9 8 7 6 5 4 3 2 1